Hello, I'm Dave. I'm a substitute Education Assistant in special education classes.

Special education serves a wide array of students, some with learning disabilities, some with emotional problems, some with physical disabilities, and more. My job varies from class to class, day to day. In most cases, I'm there to give the students extra individual attention. In autism classes I usually repeat the directions a few times and redirect students when they get distracted. In behavior problem rooms I try to keep students from getting frustrated when they don't understand something. I make sure kids with physical disabilities get access to whatever they need. I also break up fights, change diapers, open milk cartons, and monitor lunch rooms and playgrounds.

Really, though, I feel like my biggest job is to teach kids it's ok to be weird, that when you grow up you don't have to become boring or a jerk. And part of my job is trying to figure out how not to become a jerk myself, how to hang on to as many of my ethics as I can. And I guess that's what this book is about: trying to be ethical and be an adult concurrently, not in shifts.

I thought I'd work as a sub for a year or two and move on, but here I am, four years later, working on getting my own classroom. I always dreaded the idea of a career, but I think I've found something I want to do for a while. I love my job and the students with whom I've worked, with a few exceptions. As a sub, every day is something new and it's usually amazing. It's not always pleasant, but it's something I'm grateful I got to experience, something that I like to believe I'm better off for having gone through. This book chronicles my first four years as a sub. I'm not trying to say I'm great at what I do, or that I'm that I'm an expert on anything. I'm just doing the best I can and these are my stories. I hope you like them.

Thanks for reading.

S0-AFT-051

Dave

P.S.   I think it's best if you read this in intervals, preferably at school or at work, but reading it all at once at home is ok too, if that's what you want to do.

On Subbing: The First Four Years

by Dave Roche

ISBN # 9726967-5-X

This is Microcosm #76021

Second Edition, 4000 copies
October 21, 2005

Microcosm Publishing
5307 N. Minnesota Ave.
Portland OR 97217-4551
(503) 249-3826

www.microcosmpublishing.com

joe@microcosmpublishing.com

We have over 1500 other books, zines, t-shirts, patches, stickers, videos, and other things available from our catalog and on our website. Send $1 for a catalog.

At 25 I needed a change.

Leaving Los Angeles was a good first step, but I found myself falling into the same rut in my new city. I was being pulled into the quicksand of easy, low-paying jobs again. I switched from a movie theater in West Hollywood to a thrift store on West Burnside, but it was the same thing. No early mornings, no late nights, just a flat line in the middle of the day, just short of frustrating enough to do something about it. It's an easy trap to fall into, one you set for yourself with the bait, "It's only temporary."

So there I was, from noon until 9:00, selling the clothes and knick-knacks of people who had most likely died recently. Things were bad from the start. Not even a week into the job I fished a moist dollar bill from an old man's pocket. A week later a woman walked in with a pint of ice cream, bought a spoon, and started eating on her way out. She didn't even bother to wipe it off on her shirt. Even a raccoon will go through the motions of cleaning. And at least once a week, two people would almost come to blows over fake nacre earrings or a polyester blouse.

The worst part, though, was the dust. Bags of clothes that had been in attics, basements, and backs of closets for months, even years, came in every day. Our shelves were filled with picture frames, salt shakers, dishes, inspirational plaques, and candy bowls disregarded as their owners reached the termini of their lives; objects not important enough to warrant any attention in the chaos of dealing with a loved one's death. And they were all covered in dust. The dust was everywhere, making me itchy and clogging up my nose, forcing me to breathe through my mouth. About a month or so into my job I remembered I had read somewhere that dust is 80% skin cells. I was breathing in dead people. I had to get out.

But what then? I couldn't get another job I didn't care about. I needed something different. Defining myself by what I don't like and what I won't do served me well in my early 20s, but I felt I reached a point where I had to figure out what I do like. And I wanted a job where I felt like I was doing something worthwhile.

I decided to try substitute teaching. It was something I had thought about a little in Los Angeles but never got around to trying out. It sounded challenging and fun, respectable but I could still be punk. And I would be lying if I said Chris Jensen's columns in HeartattaCk and knowing that Martin from Los Crudos and John Denery were teachers didn't have some influence on my decision. I went to the main administrative building to apply. I found out, unlike California, not just anyone can be a sub in my new state. They have standards here. Without proper teaching credentials, I couldn't be a sub. I was qualified, however, to be a substitute education assistant. I didn't quite know what that was, I just knew it was like being a subtitute teacher except less pay, less responsibility, and only in special ed. rooms. I decided to go for it.

I had the easiest interview for any job I've ever applied to in my life. I only remember them asking two questions, the gist being "Are you going to abuse kids?" and "Are you a racist?" I guess my calm demeanor and huge, tolerant heart shone through in the answers I gave; I was hired. A couple days later I had to come back in to get fingerprinted. I remember washing my hands with this gritty rinseless soap. It got the ink off quickly, but left a chemical orange smell. It was strong and unpleasant, but sooned proved useful. The body odor on the bus ride to the thrift store was especially bad, even for August. I avoided it by keeping my hand close to my face and sniffing deep of the artificial oranges and thinking about how nice it was going to be to give my boss my two weeks notice.

One of my coworkers showed up drunk on my last day at the thrift store. He got sent home. My boss thought it would be a fitting goodbye to make me cash out his register as well as mine, making me stay 15 minutes late after already punching out. But I gave out so much free stuff that day I figured I was still ahead. Also, I recommend finishing a book on your last day of work. Or you should quit on the same day you read the last page. It's really satisfying. There's not much sense of accomplishment in either separately, but together they make you feel ready for a new beginning.

The week in between jobs was nerve-wracking. I felt maybe I had made a mistake. I had no qualifications for this job. What if I'm terrible at it? What if kids hate me? I tried to psych myself up for my first day, but I didn't even know when that would be. They call me in the morning to give me my assignment. I just had to lie in bed and wonder if tomorrow would be my first day. As it turned out, my first few days working in the education system were a huge let down. I got called in to work in the Talented and Gifted office. I was there 9:00 to 5:00, transcribing names and grades, collating fliers, and stuffing envelopes.

This wasn't what I wanted. This wasn't something I felt strongly about. I mean, it was better than working at the thrift store. The pay was better and I had been in the Talented and Gifted program in school, so I had some appreciation for what I was doing. Knowing that somewhere kids like me were being given the false hope that intelligence brings prestige made the job bearable, but folding paper for the first five hours and stuffing them into envelopes for last three wasn't what I had anticipated. On the second day they gave me a radio, but that didn't make things any better. They also gave me a whalebone paper folder/crease maker. That made me feel worse. I refused to use it for a while, but I figured even if I threw it back into the ocean, the whale wasn't going to come back to life. By the end of the second day I was ready for a classroom. I didn't care if I was qualified or not. If the kids hated me, well, at least it was better than using a piece of animal to fold papers while listening to static-y conservative talk radio.

A Glossary of Sorts

Here are the definitions of a few terms I use throughout this book. I hope I'm not over explaining before I even begin, but I don't want to assume everyone knows what all these mean.

The types of classes in which I work

Academic Delay Room

This is the most common type of special ed. room. It's mostly made up of kids with learning disabilities. The classes are academics based, but go at a slower pace. In the following entries, if I don't specify what kind of class I'm in, it's usually an Academic Delay Room.

Life Skills

This the room for students who function lower than the Academic Delay Room. Students with Downs Syndrome, mental retardation, autism, or other more severe learning disabilities go here. There are some academics here, but it's tied in with teaching the students how to be safe outside of school or home. In addition to the basics (addition, subtraction, and some simple multiplication and division), math consists of coin recognition and money lessons, how to read clocks, or some other number related subject that ties in directly to their lives. In lower grades there are a lot of field trips to get the kids out in public to teach them how to get around safely (crossing at the crosswalk, with the "walk sign," and so on). Higher grades are taught how to make resumés and how to conduct themselves at job interviews.

Life Skills with Nursing

These are the lowest functioning kids in the district. All the students are confined to wheelchairs, have no gross motor control or communication skills. Talking with them or reading to them rarely elicits any sort of response, although some students react favorably to loud noises or being fanned or other more sensory interactions. As there isn't any sort of academic work, I never know what I'm doing in these classrooms. There are three Life Skills with Nursing classes in the district, I believe, that are divided more by ability than by age. In the higher functioning class there are exercises to keep kids' minds stimulated, to help them understand basic cause and effect relationships. In the lowest functioning room there are exercises to strengthen the students bodies, or at least prevent them from atrophying worse.

Behavior Room

As the name would imply, this is for students with behavioral issues. There are subdivisions based on how these behaviors are manifested, but most schools don't have the resources to deal with them separately, so they get lumped into one classroom. Some kids are aggressive, getting into fights all the time, cursing at teachers or students for any perceived slight; others are good at goading other kids to fight, but don't usually fight themselves; some have ADD/ADHD and just can't sit still and be quiet long enough to function in a mainstream classroom; and others are quiet, sitting in the class probably not doing their work but not bothering anyone until someone pushes them too far.

Often these students have delays in their learning due to their behavioral issues. And it usually becomes a cycle: they're too embarrassed to admit they don't know how to read, so they act up when it's time to read and refuse to do the assignment.

Transition Class

By law, students can go to school for free until they are 21-years-old. Whereas the lower functioning students in Life Skills classes will occasionally spend an extra year (and in a few cases an extra two years) in high school, higher functioning students can go to transition classes. Transition classes are the bridge between high school and being out of school for these students. Its main focus is getting students prepared to get jobs and live on their own. In high school, students will be taught how to make a resumé or how to act in a job interview, in the transition class the teacher or the EA will sit with students indivdually and help them write their resumé, or help them fill out applications. Instead of performing mock interviews they'll help the student get a real interview. It's not all job-related. There are lessons on reading bus schedules, trips out in the community, and helping the higher functioning students go through their DMV manual so they can get their permits.

Resource Room

This is like a study hall for kids with learning disabilities. It's just a little extra help so they can keep up with the other students in their mainstream classes.

I should point out there is a good amount of crossover in these classrooms, particularly in high school. Behavior room students spend a class or two in the academic delay room, and some students spend half the day in the academic delay room and half in the Life Skills room.

A few miscellaneous terms

Autism

Autism is classified as a "pervasive developmental disorder". It was first described by Dr. Leo Kanner in 1943. One of the major features of autism is "an inability to relate to people, or any situation other than being alone." Children with autism seem to be ignoring you, but they don't intend to be rude. They're so withdrawn in themselves that it doesn't seem like they are aware someone is talking to them. They also tend not to flinch or react to loud, sudden noises. This condition is present from birth, although autism is seldom diagnosed before two or three years of age. Because babies with autism don't coo, fret, reach out, or ask for attention they are seen as well behaved. But they avoid social interaction and rapidly fall behind in social development.

Communication deficits are another major feature of autism. Half of all autistic children never learn to speak. Those that do often just echo what they hear, sometimes with a delay of hours or even weeks before they repeat a phrase. Pronoun reversal is another common speech abnormality. Autistic children refer to themselves as "he/she", "you", or by name. This is linked to echolalia.

Even before the period in which language is usually acquired, autistic children show deficits in communication. They don't babble as much as other children, and their babbling conveys less information.

Autistic Children often exhibit abnormal "compulsive and ritualistic" movements. Hand flapping, toe walking, twirling, rocking back and forth, and lip smacking are some of the more common examples.

Choosing
Choosing means free time. Kids get to choose what they want to do, hence choosing.

Shaving cream table
The shaving cream table is, as you would guess, a table covered with shaving cream. No surprise there. It's used in autism/communication behaviors rooms. It's a tactile thing for the students and they generally respond to it well. Beans, sand, and shredded paper are some of the materials used on tables in other autism rooms.

My First Year

September 2000
to
June 2001

Cope-Grey Middle School
September 8

I've seen teachers flinch upon hearing the name of this school, treating me with a mixture of respect and sympathy usually reserved for returning soldiers when I tell them my first assignment was in the Behavior Room here.

Within the first half hour a kid asked me if I was a hippie. I thought that was a little odd, but it was a question that followed me to four or five other schools. Within the next half hour a kid asked me if I wanted to fight. He wasn't particularly threatening, but he wasn't joking either. When I declined he asked why not. I said, "I don't want to lose my job." He was satisfied with that.

I helped kids with their grammar worksheets the first half of the day. Basically, I begged the kids to pay attention to me, then gave them the answers. The second half of the day was spent breaking up fights. I should have got a lunch break in between but the teacher I ws working with screwed me over. I had planned on using that half hour to run home, put on deodorant (which I forgot to put on that morning, making me really self-conscious) and drop a sweet number two I'd been brewing all day. (I refuse to poop at work, even in the teachers' bathroom.) Instead, I had to walk around the cafeteria and make sure kids didn't throw carrots at each other.

By the end of the day the kids were cool with me. I think it was because I played basketball with them. And probably because I didn't get them in trouble for cursing. They asked if I was coming back on Monday. "I don't know. Should I?" I love making kids, especially middle schoolers who think they're bad-asses, admit they like me, no matter how quietly they say it.

Transition Class
September 15

I worked in a transition class on the university campus. I conducted one-on-one goal meetings with students. We chose one of the goals from their individualized folder (every student in special ed. has a file that explains what the student is capable of and what his or her academic, social, and behavioral goals are) and discussed how to achieve it. This was only my second classroom assignment and I felt grossly underqualified to be working unsupervised, one-on-one with students. After one 45-minute meeting with a student, all we figured out was that she liked Disney movies.

Bernard Elementary School
September 20, 21

This was a behavior class for first and second graders. The kids tried to act tough but were too young to pull it off. They were aloof and had tons of attitude, but when things didn't go their way they'd cry.

The biggest problem in this class was kids running away. To compound the problem, this was a portable classroom; once kids got out the door they were outside. One kid ran and wasn't found for an hour. He was 30 blocks away. Most of the time, though, kids would just run out and stand by the door or hang out by the dumpster. It was my job to follow them out. I was told to try to coax them in, but don't yell or demand anything. One kid decided to take his anger out on me. When I tried to talk he yelled, "Shut up, bitch... Shut up, butthead." I wanted to explain to him that the key to insulting is escalation. "Shut up, bitch" is more offensive than "Shut up, butthead" and should therefore come after. I decided that was probably a fourth grade concept.

Lakeside Middle School
September 27-29

Middle schools are generally the worst places in the world, both for students and for subs. I went to this behavior problem class fully expecting to leave a broken man. I was pleasantly surprised.

I won the kids' trust early. A girl ran out of the room and I followed her. At first she didn't want me around, but she opened up to me and told me what she didn't like about school. She made a lot of sense and I ended up agreeing with her. Then I told her what I didn't like about schools.

The nice thing about being a sub is that I get to go in and joke around with the kids. I rarely have to be the bad guy that gives detentions or referrals or even time-outs. I bet the kids I could get the answers to their math problems as fast as their calculators and I did my stupid "stab myself in the eye with my glasses" trick. The kids told me they wished I was their new teacher. It was flattering, but I knew they liked me like this just because I was a sub. On the second day a kid actually gave me an apple. I didn't think this ever happened outside of black and white movies. I wished he had a slingshot in his back pocket or a frog under his hat. That would have made the picture complete.

Polk High School
October 2

A girl laughed in my face.

The McDougal Center
October 4

The McDougal Center is a place for abused kids. It's a whole compound set up with two buildings that housed all the kids about 50 yards away from the school. Before class, the teacher (who bore a strong resemblance to Ben Stiller) warned me that I shouldn't hug any of the students, it might trigger traumatic memories.

I ate my lunch on the grass at the edge of the playground. I felt so sad I almost cried. These kids probably almost never leave this two or three block area. They had been messed up so bad that not only were they taken from their homes, but they couldn't even be hugged. I got five bites into my lunch and couldn't eat anymore. I dumped the rest in the bushes and prepared myself for three more hours.

Hanson Elementary School
October 5, 6

There were six students in the class. Including me, there were four adults, one of whom looked like a bigger version of Gallagher. Things went smoothly until PE. All the special ed. students in the school were put together for PE. It was a bad idea: 18 kids, some with emotional problems, some with behavioral problems, some with autism, all in the same room, competing. A kid thought he wasn't getting his fair share of turns and flipped out. He started swearing (well, saying "frickin'") and tears of rage welled up in his eyes. He threw his shirt in a teacher's face and his shoes at a student. Another EA asked if he wanted to go into the hall and talk about it. He yelled, "Shut your piehole!" Piehole? Why would a 7-year-old kid say piehole ever, much less in the throes of such intense anger and frustration?

Two hours later a kid knocked my glasses off my face and told me my breath stank while I tried to help him read.

Van Buren High School
October 9

I helped kids steam vegetables and make grilled cheeses. A girl in the class flirted with me, which was very, very uncomfortable.

Then I worked one-on-one with a student who kept repeating things. I must have heard him say, "I'm going to be a cheerleader for Halloween" at least 30 times. He also told me repeatedly he wanted to be a cop when he grew up. That was also uncomfortable.

Transition Class
October 10

My second assignment at the transition class on the university campus was much easier than my first. I took the class to the library. The whole walk across campus I was thinking, "I hope nobody thinks I'm *in* this class." I tried to figure out how to make myself look not like a special ed. student. I'm not proud of that.

Lowery Elementary School
October 16-19

One of the kids looked like a miniature version of a stand-up comic from the 80's. He had a little mullet and wore suspenders. I think he was made somewhere deep in Bud Friedman's laboratory.

On Wednesday I got to go with the class on a field trip to a pumpkin patch on Sauvie Island. There was a one-eyed dog there.

Polk High School
October 20

I worked in the behavior room today. First period I was led to a windowless room in the basement and was told I'd lead a reading lesson with a few kids down there by myself. You can guess how it went.

I went back to the classroom for the rest of the day. There was a sub for the other EA, too. She thought I was a student and kept trying to help me with math. I let it go on for about half an hour before I told her.

Transition Class
October 27

Before class the other EA and I talked about activism. I had run into him at a protest against the IMF and then again at Food Not Bombs. He gave me the lowdown on how not to look like an infiltrator. He stopped talking when the teacher came in.

The class went on a field trip to a community center for a

Halloween party with two other transition classes. It was awesome. Most of the kids were dressed up. I saw Pebbles, Zorro, a princess, a wolfman, and some animal masks. Aside from one kid who was miserable and kept asking me to box him in the ring next door, everyone was having a great time. One student did a hyperkinetic dance to some boy band. I thought it was kind of funny. In general, I spent a lot of time smirking and feeling superior. Then I noticed all the kids were dancing and having fun and loving life and there I was, standing against the wall by myself thinking, "They could at least have some vegan candy at this stupid party." That's when I realized I'm the worst person in the world.

Newton Elementary School
November 3

This was a regular ed. class. There wasn't even an autistic kid for me to work with. It was a pretty easy day.

Some kids got busted for trying to write dirty words during reading. One wrote "dum bisc," which the teacher and I assumed was "dumb bitch". The other kid wrote "eugle ass mothe fouche." The working theory is that the first word is "ugly". I suggested they should write it correctly 100 times and have their parents sign it. The teacher thought I was joking.

There was an assembly on building character led by Ronald McDonald. I spent the next hour with my jaw clenched and my fist balled up.

Fairfax Elementary School
November 6

Between getting called to work late and the #30 bus taking forever, I got to school three hours late. The teacher was a little upset. She didn't want me there and let me know it. She said I wasn't needed, and I had to agree as there were only two students and now three adults. She was really rude and tried to get rid of me. When she found out I have a college degree and I don't smoke, she turned around completely. She was really nice to me and told me she was going to try to get me a permanent position in the class. No thanks.

Harrison High School
November 15

A student told me I look like Mr. Mitchell, Dennis the Menace's dad.

That's easily the nicest comment I've gotten on my appearance from a student.

Clouster Elementary School
November 17, 20-22, 27-30

This was a fourth and fifth grade behavior problem class. One of the students was a textbook example of ADHD. I'm not exaggerating when I say I never saw him sit still for more than a minute and a half the entire time I was there. Another kid would be nice for a little while, then the teacher would ask him to be quiet and he'd go crazy. "No, you shut up! You're an idiot!" No matter what the teacher did next (which was usually ask him to take a time out) he'd swear at her then knock things over, like chairs or the little blackboard. After my second day there I had a dream in which I swore at him, knocked him down, and was about to beat him up when I woke up. Though troubling, it was very cathartic.

Another kid was really dramatic about everything. I liked telling him about my veganism because he couldn't understand it. "You don't even eat *bacon*?!? What's the matter with you?"

I talked with a couple students during recess. They were lying to me, but not in the "let's trick the sub" way. It was more pathological lying. One kid told me his uncle had a peg leg and his grandfather had a glass eye. The other told me he once broke a rottweiler's neck. His family threw the dog's body in the dump.

Back in the classroom, I sat with the kids on the carpet while waiting for free time. A few looked at me and started giggling. Obnoxious, but no big deal; I'm used to that. Then more giggling and pointing. I was starting to get upset when I realized the way I was sitting caused my pants to bulge up, looking like I had a huge boner. I didn't know what to do. I couldn't say, "That's not funny," because it was funny. I mean, not to me; I was upset. But, had that happened to one of my teachers when I was a kid, I would have laughed. I couldn't make a joke out of it, which is what I'd do around adults. The best I could manage was to straighten my pants and say, "You guys, it's my pants. And that's not appropriate."

My last day there everything blew up. When I turned off the radio after first break was over a girl yelled, "Turn that back on, you faggot." Later, with about 45 minutes left in the day, I took the kids out for recess. The girl asked me to hold her watch. I thought she didn't want to lose it while she played. Really, she wanted me to protect it so she could kick some kid's ass. That fight started a chain reaction. We'd just get one fight under control and another would break out. Some of the kids had to be carried out of the room and taken to their bus early. In the confusion, the girl forgot her watch. I didn't, but I didn't give it back. That's what a homophobic slur will cost you, kid.

(I had intended to give her the watch the next day when things had calmed down, when I could make more of a point of it, that even though she had insulted me I was still going to do the right thing and give it back. But I got called to a different school.)

DuBois Middle School
December 1, 4

What a nightmare. Another behavior problem class. There was a sub for the teacher as well as me. She had some sort of weird power issues and totally screwed up the class. I'm no expert, but in a class full of kids from questionable homes and fragile senses of identity, coupled with the onset of puberty, you don't go in and demand respect, change a bunch of rules (stupid stuff like refusing to let students sit in the chair with wheels) and ignore the kids when they try to help you keep the day going as close to what they're used to as possible. It's also bad form to keep a kid after school to yell at him and end it with, "I hope you miss your bus."

Needless to say, there was a lot of tension all day. I've never heard so much abusive language in such a small period of time. And the students didn't confine their anger to the sub. A fight broke out and one student tried to choke another. Things only calmed down when the other EA and I took the class down to the gym to play basketball. They didn't earn it, but we had given up on everything else. Surprisingly no fights broke out and the day ended calmly, although I don't know if I'll be able to get that sweaty adolescent gym smell out of my sweater.

Riverton Elementary School
December 7, 8, 11

I girl I worked with took an immediate disliking to me. She ordered me to read her report on wolves. I couldn't figure out what the word "sml" was supposed to be. I guessed "small", but I was wrong and she got really upset. I asked her to talk to me politely and she threatened to bite me if I didn't continue reading. Then she said she'd scream if I didn't tell her how to spell a word. Five-and-a-half hours left.

When she started bothering other students the teacher took her out to the hall to talk. I was left in charge of the rest of the class. I was to read from a joke book, but it was so unfunny I couldn't do it. I let the kids tell their own jokes. I proved I am master of the fake laugh.

On Monday I worked one-on-one with a different student in a different class. It was a lot easier. This kid just needed a lot of refocusing. For the last hour the class made Christmas cards. I manned the hot glue gun in case the Elmers proved useless against pipe cleaners. The teacher played music. She had a bunch of great CDs: Louis Armstrong, Frank Sinatra, Ella Fitzgerald, Tommy Dorsey, Miles Davis, Duke Ellington, etc. She only played one tape over and over: Kenny G's Christmas album. I came dangerously close to hot gluing my ears shut.

Transition Class
December 12
This was the creepiest day ever. The class went on a field trip to the mall. I accompanied a student to a video store where he bought softcore porn. A little later a student ran out into the middle of the ice-skating rink and started masturbating. Luckily the teacher took care of that, but I caught him masturbating a couple times after that and had to stop him. I would just start talking to him about anything and he'd stop, but not for very long.

Bernard Elementary School
January 4,5
I got called to the fourth and fifth grade behavior room. A fight broke out during recess. I took one of the combatants out for a walk around the school to calm him down. We circled the school for an hour and a half. He told me about his life. "No one's ever kept a promise. Everyone always lies to me."

I said, "I've never lied to you."

He eyed me suspiciously. "You've never promised me anything!" I tried to think of something simple but meaningful I could promise him that I could deliver within the last hour of the day. I failed.

Hillary Center
January 9
The Hillary Center is a pre-kindergarten school for lower function-

ing kids with autism or mental retardation. I experienced two firsts today: My first toileting duties (I had to help a kid take off his overalls and diaper, get on the toilet, then dress him again) and my first kick to the testicles.

Kennedy High School
January 12

It's funny how I still feel uncomfortable in high school gyms, especially during square dancing.

Tyler High School
January 19

I helped a kid read. His voice cracked and he got really embarrassed. It was heartbreaking. Two girls in the back of the class developed crushes on me. They wrote me notes. It was uncomfortable.

Mersey Elementary School
January 22

I worked one-on-one with a girl with Downs Syndrome. She was really sweet and polite and had great social skills, well beyond other kids her age. I helped her with math. She wasn't getting the concept at all. She dropped back in her chair and said she hated herself for not knowing big words or how to do math. She knew she had Downs Syndrome and she knew what that meant, but she hadn't learned how to deal with it. I didn't know what to do. Goddammit, what happened to the easy days of helping kids shit and getting kicked in the balls? I was sitting right next to this girl who needed someone to prove to her she was awesome and I didn't know how to do it. I felt smothered by my own ineffectiveness. I told her being good at math and knowing big words isn't everything, she had a good sense of humor and knew how to introduce me to people and that counted for something. I think I made her feel a little better, but I don't think what I said had any lasting effect.

Freeman Middle School
January 25

I went to pick up the kids from the bus but the driver wouldn't open the door until I knocked and explained who I was. She thought I was a student. This was a middle school.

I went with a student to his mainstream health class. Today's lesson was on birth control and the teacher passed around different contraceptives for the class to look at. You're in a bad position when you find yourself saying, "OK, you've had it long enough, pass it along," to a kid staring at a diaphragm.

Polk High School
January 26

There were news cameras around as I walked in to school. To try to synopsize the situation: a while back there was a lot of tension between the Polk Principal and the superintendent. Polk had the worst record for academic achievement and the highest student drop out rate in the city. It's also the poorest school. The principal was doing a good job of turning things around, but was getting no support from the superintendent and the administration. These conditions caused him to take a couple months sick leave due to stress. This was his first day back and the students were lining the halls to show support. The superintendent was also there to make nice-nice in front of the cameras.

Anyway, I was in the resource room, which is kind of like a study hall for special ed. students. This was finals time, so there wasn't much for me to do. I had hall duty, which meant I wandered the halls reading *Maggie Cassidy* and asking the occasional student, "Do you have a hall pass?" I didn't really pay attention to their answers because I wasn't going to bust them anyway.

After lunch was make-up tests, so the school was pretty empty. I helped a teacher put together work folders for students. "Do you like music, Mr. Roche?" Sure. He put on a tape for me and left the room. I spent the next hour and a half collating papers while listening to Pachelbel's *Canon in D* eight times in a row.

Polk High School
February 1, 2, 5-9

I had a week and a half assignment in the behavior problem class. I was supposed to work one-on-one with a different student each period, going over a reading lesson with them at the back of the room. Either due to a learning disability or just not caring, these students were reading at a third grade level. And they were too embarrassed to admit they couldn't read, so they skipped the reading lessons. On Tuesday a record was set: three of the five students showed up. Actually, a fourth student showed up, but he left before it was time for me to work with him. A student wanted to talk about girls after his reading lesson. I was worried, but his questions were pretty tame, like how do you ask a girl out. Oh, the irony of my giving advice on how to ask a girl out.

"What if she says no?"

"Well, you leave her alone and look for someone else to ask out."

"What if you really want to go out with her?"

"No, you have to leave her alone."

The next day he asked me questions about work. "What if someone accidentally breaks something, should he tell his boss?"

Hillary Center

February 26

At recess I picked kids up and pretended I was going to throw them over the fence. They loved it, although I'm not so sure the teacher would have approved of it.

For the p.m. class I worked one-on-one with a severely autistic boy. The first hour I was to do color and shape matching exercises with him while he wore headphones. The teacher told me the music he was listening to was supposed to have some effect on his brain to make it work more neurotypically. She warned me strongly not to listen to it, that it would mess with my brain. What would it do? Would it make me super-normal? Psychic? Would it make me like Rush? I couldn't wait for her to leave the room.

Working with the student went something like this: ask the him to perform some task, like stacking blocks or sorting plastic rings by size; ask him 10 to 20 more times as he stared right through me; sink back in my chair and sigh as I realize I'm totally blowing it; stay silent for 30 to 45 seconds as I try to figure out what to do; ask him a few more times; switch to some other task. This cycle generally lasted around 5 minutes and was repeated for two and a half hours. Luckily the teacher was off running errands, so no one saw what a total failure I was. She came back with five minutes left in class. "How'd it go?" "It was a little rough, but I think it went alright."

I felt bad about my performance that day, but even worse, on the way home I realized I never listened to that music.

Zulueta Middle School

February 28

Second period was prep period - no students. I sat alone in the classroom reading when I felt the ground start to shake. I wasn't sure if it was an earthquake or just some vestigial Los Angeles paranoia. As the shaking continued you could hear the school fall silent. Then, after the briefest of pauses, the kids went crazy. Squeals of fear were drowned out by boys yelling, "Earthquake!" I stuck my head out the door to see if anybody was evacuating. No. It was nothing like the earthquake drills. From what I could see, not only were kids not under their desks, they weren't even in their classrooms. It was like watching a life-size version of one of those old electric football games; kids were bouncing around the halls. Kids who would have been making fun of my glasses not ten minutes ago were running up to me excitedly asking, "Did you feel that? That was an earthquake!"

The rest of the day went as well as can be expected after a disruption like that.

Hillary Center
March 8

I worked one-on-one with a kid in the p.m. class. I found out the reason they needed a sub today was because this kid had head-butted the regular EA's jaw and sent her to the hospital. Awesome. I escaped with my jaw intact, but I did receive two blows to the testicles. The first was when I was trying to get my student ready to go home. He was kind of flipping out. I tried to put his shoes back on. Apparently he doesn't like shoes. He also doesn't like my nuts. The second time I was putting him in his car seat. That's when I quit, went to the office and checked out.

Clouster Elementary School
March 13

I returned to a class in which I subbed for two weeks last semester. I was greeted with a few smiles and an "Oooh, you're ugly!" There was a new girl in the classroom. The teacher told me I couldn't be alone with her, because if she got mad at me she might tell her dad I touched her.

Zulueta Middle School
March 14

This was a Life Skills with Nursing class. These classes are for the lowest functioning kids in the district. The kids are all in wheelchairs, have no gross motor control, and are nonverbal. They really can't express themselves in any way. Occasionally they'll laugh, but it's rarely in response to something that is happening to them. It's unknown if they're oblivious to what's going on around them or are aware but trapped in bodies that won't let them express themselves. I was already really depressed and feeling like

I was in way over my head and the day hadn't even started yet.

The first job of the day was to change all the students' diapers. There are kids as old as seventeen in this class. Another assistant and I had to lift the boys on to a changing table then strap them down. The other assistant did all changing with the first two boys. I stood back and occasionally handed him a diaper or a wipe. He had me change the third boy. I opened the diaper. It was full of shit. I gagged and dropped the tape of the diaper on to the kid's pubic hair. Something about noticing the kid's pubic hair made me really sad. I can't explain it, except I guess I realized these students were entering adulthood and what kind of lives could they lead? Does this kid know what's going on? Does he have any of the crippling self-consciousness that hits all boys that age as he lies there naked and immobile while a total stranger tries to delicately remove tape from his pubic hair without pulling any out and without touching him? My body was tense trying not to gag and I kept thinking, "If I can just hold out a couple hours I can find a nice alley where I can cry on my lunch break."

The teacher was a very nice woman in her early 50s. She sang and played guitar for the students. She played "Zippity-Doo-Dah", "Blue Suede Shoes", "(You Ain't Nothin' but a) Hound Dog", and a few others. She only played guitar on the downbeats and she added a lot of her own vocal inflections, some of which were in tune. They asked me to play guitar. "Play something and we'll sing. Do you know any Elvis songs?"

"No."

"How 'bout 'Rock Around the Clock'?"

"Uh, no, sorry." The only songs I know how to play are by The Ramones and Jawbreaker. I might remember how to play a Minor Threat song once I got started, but I didn't think those were appropriate. One of the other EAs found a keyboard that had a bunch of preset songs. They played "La Vida Loca" three times in a row and everyone danced, pushing the chairs around and singing in the kids' faces. I have to admit I was having a good time. It was good to see adults do something ridiculous and fun without any hint of self-consciousness, and the kids picked up on it. They couldn't sing or dance or clap, but they were rocking back and forth and laughing. I no longer felt sad but totally energized. At the end of the day I felt as though I had been through some sort of profound and inarticulable experience.

Shore Elementary School
March 19, 20

This was a pre-kindergarten class. I had to change a diaper. I did a really sloppy job and smeared shit on the changing mat. I felt queasy. I had the kid stand up so I could pull up and button his pants. He was having a hard time balancing and kept trying to steady himself by grabbing my glasses.

Bernard Elementary School
March 21

Things started badly. Kids ran into the classroom calling each other names and throwing chocolate chips at each other. Even if your child doesn't have ADHD, please don't give him or her chocolate chips for breakfast. Later a kid threatened to sue me because I picked him up off the floor.

Polk High School
March 22

As I walked to work I thought about how much I liked this school, about how the kids thought I was a weirdo at first but they grew to like me, and I get a warm greeting every time I come here now. I felt confident. As soon as I walked through the door someone made fun of my glasses.

I was working with a student in the library when the assistant principal interrupted to chastise him. Apparently this kid was given a half day in-school suspension, so he went AWOL for a little while. The AP was angry. He ended his diatribe with, "If you think it's a good idea to get around a half-day suspension by skipping school for three days, you're stupider than I thought." He took off and left me to deal with the student. Luckily things didn't go too bad. I think it's because when the student called the assistant principal an asshole, he could see I agreed, even though I had to say, "Watch your language, please."

Transition Class
April 4

Watching a kid in a wheelchair get hit in the head with a basketball is intensely unpleasant.

Clouster Elementary School
April 10

I didn't get called to work on Thursday, only got a half day on Friday, didn't get called on Monday and didn't get called today. I was starting to get paranoid. Were they firing me in some passive way? Why wasn't I working anymore? Did my boss get a hold of my last zine? If they stop giving me assignments can I get unemployment? Will I have to look for another job? Never in my life did I think I would call my boss and ask why I had the day off, but there you go. I found out my boss was sick and there was a sub for her. She didn't realize she hadn't called me.

I subbed for a secretary today. I passed the room in which I subbed before on my way to the office. The kids stuck their heads out and said hello. "Are you gonna be in here today?"

"No, I'm subbing for the secretary today."

"OK, I'll get in trouble so I can get sent down to the office to see you."

My day mostly consisted of answering the sporadic calls that interrupted my reading *Cannery Row*. Usually the person would call and ask for a teacher. I'd put her/him on hold, read a paragraph of my book, then pick up the phone and say, "I'm sorry s/he's busy with students right now. Can I take a message?" My only other duty was handing out band-aids.

Thompson Middle School
April 11

Today was nice and relaxed. The teacher was laid back. He showed me some pictures: loving photographs of his guitar resting tenderly against a tree. It would have been sweet if it weren't vaguely creepy.

I had to coax a kid into doing his clock assignment. The teacher would announce a time and the class had to arrange the hands on cardboard clock faces. He refused to do it. "I'm too smart for this," he kept protesting.

"Come on, let me see you do one. I don't know how smart you are." After five minutes of trying to talk him into it, he reluctantly did one and showed it to me. I moved the clock hands so it was the wrong answer. "This isn't even close! Try again." He giggled and did it again. I messed it up again. "Wrong again. Here, try a different one - 4:30." He showed me 4:30 and I messed it up. "Nope. I thought you said you were too smart for this."

He giggled and put it back to 4:30. I got him to do the whole assignment this way.

Branum Middle School
April 12

I spent the first two hours of the day working in the main office. This was the moment I'd been waiting for: I was given access to kids' permanent records. I could lose this kid's detention slips, or change that kid's 'F' to a 'B'. In the end I didn't change anything. Fuck 'em, they're probably going to make fun of my glasses the second I step into the hall. (I was wrong, they made fun of my ears.) I just put photo stickers on folders. Some of the these were stamped 'CUM FOLDER'. Sure, I'm a jerk for snickering at that, but not as big a jerk as the guy who couldn't think of a better abbreviation for 'cumulative'. While in the office I drank just enough tepid coffee to have bad breath and a desperate urge to urinate, then went to class. I gave the kids a spelling test.

Kennedy High School
April 25

I worked one-on-one with a student with whom I had worked a few times before. He kept asking, "Do you remember me?" and telling me how much he missed me. It was nice. But when I made him clean up his mess after cooking I heard him say under his breath, "I hate your guts."

I came back from my lunch break to catch the end of a lesson on hearing loss. The teacher told the class, "The number one thing that damages hearing-- actually there are two number one things." The first was "rock music." As soon as she said that I expected Twisted Sister to enter the room and blow all the papers off her desk with sheer rock force.

The other number one thing was loud machinery.

Shore Elementary School
May 1

A girl told me I was her best friend, then I almost broke her arm.

Taft High School
April 30 - June 8

For the last two months of the year I subbed in the Life Skills class. It was OK. The teacher was a little hard to handle. She had a very exact way of doing things, but didn't explain what that way was until I had already done it wrong. Everything she said was urgent, but she'd often change her mind. It wasn't uncommon for her to send me to the office for something and by the time the secretary could show me where it was the other EA would come down to tell me to forget about it. The other EA was nice enough. He seemed really normal. He liked top 40 rock, wore Nike sandals, just the average mid 20s white guy. He didn't get along with the teacher and she didn't like him. When either was alone with me they'd complain about the other.

The students were great. One kid was close to nonverbal. He was good humored and made up for not being able to speak by expressing himself through really exaggerated motions. One day he gave me a high five and acted like he hurt his hand. He ran around shaking it, then kissed it. It was very Harpo Marx.

May 3

The class went on a field trip to a Mexican restaurant for Cinco De Mayo. I tried to make it clear to the staff that I wasn't a student, but when the bass player for the mariachi band made funny faces at me when they played "Tutti Frutti" I knew I had failed. Dribbling water on myself didn't help any.

May 7

I played dominoes with a girl. The teacher pulled me aside and warned me to be careful around her, she might do "sexual things". She never explained what that meant.

May 8

We took a field trip to the Rhododendron Gardens. A girl insisted that a duck with a blue bill was a platypus. I had a hard time convincing her otherwise.

May 16

The teacher gave a student a referral for farting. It didn't even make a noise, it was just pungent. "You do that in the bathroom." Later the teacher asked if I was coming back next week in front of the class. "I don't know. Maybe. Should I?" They all yelled that I should. I'm shameless. Then the teacher said she was feeling kind of sick and the whole class told her to stay at home. I win.

May 23

In front of the whole class, the teacher asked a kid, "Your hair is dirty. Did you shower today?" When the student said she had, the teacher said, "No you didn't. Let me smell your hair." She made the student go home, take a shower, and come back.

May 31

A student from another class asked me what grade I was in. I told him I was a senior.

June 6

For the past couple weeks I was the one working most with a student who had to be constantly monitored. I was the only staff he liked, mostly because I was the gentlest, least invasive person there. When I had to follow him in to the bathroom, I'd wash my hands or fix my hair instead of stand and wait for him. It's a little thing, but it means a lot. The teacher would tell him to do something and he'd sit and glare at her. I'd give him a few seconds and say, "OK, c'mon, let's go," and he'd do it. He was a tough kid to get close to, but I could tell he trusted me and he knew I gave him the respect others hadn't. I can't begin to explain how horrible I felt today when I learned he had to be constantly monitored because he was a sexual assaulter.

June 8

The other EA wasn't in today. The teacher was upset that he didn't call her up to tell her he wasn't coming in. She called his house at 8:30 a.m. to yell at him, while he was sick.

I took the kids outside for lunch. A girl pointed out two squirrels on the roof of a shed. When the rest of the class looked, the squirrels became amorous.

I am a good shoplifter, or at least I was until I quit. I found this out the summer following my first year of subbing. It was a discovery borne of necessity.

I thought I could coast through those three months on my meager savings. I had enough to cover rent until school started up again, but not much more. I figured I could scrape by. I mean, really, who needs money? Food Not Bombs serves four days a week and I had coffee hook-ups for the other three. That worked for a while. I'd scam my way onto a bus downtown (my monthly bus pass being a credit card-sized portrait of a Boston terrier that happened to be the same colors as the real passes), hang out at the library until I was hungry, then hop on the streetcar to the coffeeshop where my friend worked. There I'd drink coffee until the hunger pangs turned to nausea. That night maybe I'd have some rice or pasta or Food Not Bombs bread until the next free feed.

Eventually it caught up to me. I had to eat at least as much as the constant intake of coffee made me shit. I sold all the CDs I was willing to part with and I still was broke. I couldn't bring myself to sell plasma. [I'm not passing judgment on anyone who sells plasma, because A) what I ended up doing could hardly count as taking some sort of moral high ground, and B) I ended up selling plasma two years later to help fund my trip to Australia. It was bad, and not because of the actual process of having my plasma leaked out of me, but because of the regulars at the clinic. Try as I might to bury myself in J.D. Salinger's *22 Stories,* I got stuck talking to people. The chill of having my blood pumped back into my body with room temperature saline instead of body temperature plasma didn't compare to the shiver that ran through me when someone who I figured to be the Cliff Claven of Alpha Plasma, upon realizing he didn't recognize my face, referred to me as "fresh fish."] So I started shoplifting.

I didn't want to, but I was afraid if I didn't eat more my body would find something else to shit out, like bone marrow or maybe childhood memories. One day I'd look into the toilet and there would be the time some guy gave me a Ziggy poster because I banged my head pretty hard and started crying at his yard sale. I set out guidelines for ethical shoplifting: I would only take from huge, sketchy corporations; I would only take things I would want to support (because those products still make money); and I would only take what I need.

I took to shoplifting quite naturally, as one with an innate talent might take to chess. My first attempts, although effective, lacked finesse, but I got better quickly. As my talents grew, so did my definition of "need". I grew to enjoy shoplifting and continued to do it after I started working again. In fact, I took secret delight in shoplifting during my lunch breaks.

I had a hard time justifying it after a while. When I nearly got busted by a student I felt awfully low. I was going to give it up, but I had a good idea. A perfect opportunity to overlap my deadbeat style with my responsible adult life arose and I couldn't pass it up.

I had a two week assignment at this really good elementary school in a poorer part of town. They had a free bread program for the families and had pamphlets on how one could regain the right to vote after being convicted of a felony. They were doing really good community-minded things, so of course they were underfunded. They were so underfunded, in fact, the teachers had to put up wish lists in the halls, asking parents to help them acquire supplies. It was ridiculous, there was nothing on those lists a school should have to do without, and, aside from the digital camera, there was nothing expensive. It was mostly things like colored pencils or markers.

I wrote down everything on the lists and made fliers out of it. There were two shows over the four day weekend in the middle of my stint there, one at which I read and a punk show at my house. At both I passed out the fliers and asked everyone who shoplifts to help me steal everything on this list.

I had all these justifications for why this wasn't wrong: corporations should be donating this stuff, so really, we're just acting as the little angels on their shoulders without them knowing it, or punks were using their white privilege to help kids of color, but really it just came down to this: shoplifting is fun and we were going to do it anyway.

The punks came through. At the end of the four days we had 16 packages of markers, 6 sets of colored pencils, 5 Spanish/English dictionaries, 5 measuring tapes, 3 ink cartridges, 2 jump ropes, a ream of purple paper and a Magnadoodle. I biked to work early the next morning, snuck into the teachers' lounge and spread everything out on the table with a note reading, "Here are some gifts from the Punks."

Maybe what I did was wrong, but seeing the PE teacher walk down the hall with jump ropes I stole just 12 hours ago feels a way better than voting on some ballot measure.

My Second Year

September 2001
to
June 2002

Thurston Elementary School
Sept. 5-11

My first assignment back was at an after school program for home-less kids in first through fifth grades. Within my first five minutes of being back with students someone asked me if my nose was real. I told him it wasn't, but after the fifth time he asked me to take it off I broke down and told him the truth.

Since this was an after school program, it was more relaxed. The day would start with a snack and then go into art. The art project was simple the first day, it just involved cutting and gluing stuff. A kid told me his brother sometimes stabs people. His brother was also in the class; he was cutting his ruler with his scissors. I made sure I was an arm's distance away when I asked him to stop.

Recess was next and I played football. Two kids tackled me and I suffered a grass stain on my right knee. That's when I opted out of the game. I checked on the kids on the tire swing. The potential stabber followed me around. He said he once brought a knife to school and that he wanted to kill himself. He also said, "My mother's life would be better if I wasn't born." I said that wasn't true and that he was probably the most important thing in his mother's life.

The next day I worked one-on-one with a student out in the hall. Mostly he played with an electronic Mr. Potatohead game or a plastic shark. All I had to do was keep him calm and get him to sit down when he thought his shark wanted to swim around the halls.

I played football at recess, but again it got too rough. These kids live in homeless shelters and they don't get a lot of attention there. When someone does interact and listen and play with them, they really appreciate it. Sometimes they get a little overzealous in the way they show their appreciation. So I left to push kids on swings. One of the kids (who migrated from the football game) threatened to punch me in the crunchies if I didn't push him higher.

There was a lot of tension and whispering between the teacher and the principal as we got the kids ready for the bus. The buses took off without the kid who said he wished he wasn't born and his brother. It turns out their mother abandoned them; she snuck out in the middle of the night, leaving them in the homeless shelter.

Harrison High School
September 12, 13

I worked in the behavior room today. One of the students was having a hard time and the teacher said he could take a walk around the school to calm down, but I'd have to go with him. He hated me before we even left the room, but he really hated me when I took his water bottle away. He kept spilling water all over the stairs and the halls. I couldn't let him do that. He threatened to tackle me on the stairs if I didn't give it back, but I called his bluff. I gave it back to him when we returned to the classroom. Then he ran away. The teacher asked me to look for him. I took my time wandering the halls. By the time I got back to the room the rest of the class had turned on one girl. I guess they made fun of her pretty bad; she was sitting in the hall near tears. I tried to comfort her.

Polk High School
September 14

There was a pep rally after lunch. The principal took over for the last 15 minutes, led the pledge of allegiance (which I refused to recite) and talked about what had just happened in New York and DC. He went in to a speech about how World War III is upon us and some of the kids might be asked to serve their country.

DiMarco Elementary School
September 20

I got called to the PM kindergarten class. I slept in until 11:00, and when I got to work at noon, the teacher told me to take a half hour lunch break. With such an auspicious beginning, I thought I was in for an easy day. And things did go smoothly until the end of recess. I had to get a kid who refused to come in. I grabbed his hand and he dropped to the ground. I tried to get him to his feet but he went limp. He was a big kid and I didn't want to throw my back out carrying him up the stairs. I kind of lifted him, braced myself behind him and tried to push him up the stairs. It was a spectacular failure and it probably would have been funny had the fire alarm not gone off when I got him halfway up. I thought he'd be excited to get to go back outside, but no, he was still limp. It wouldn't have been so hard to get him out, as this time I had gravity on my side, but the teacher gave me a second kid to take outside. He was eager to get outside, but covered his eyes as he made his way down the stairs. He'd take a step or two, then fall over, take another step, fall. I begged him to uncover his eyes to no avail. My left arm was constantly lifting one kid up and my right arm was dragging the other. It was unbelievably frustrating.

After that, the rest of my day was spent tying shoes and trying to avoid the shaving cream table.

Torres Elementary School
September 21

This class was great: the kids were nice and the teachers were friendly. I played kickball with kids then helped them make patterns with blocks. I spent my lunch in the teachers' lounge, away from the other teachers, reading, as I spend almost all my lunch breaks. This one was cut short, however, when I heard the principal say, through someone's walkie-talkie, "Where's Jackie's sub? We need him out here." I guess I was supposed to be on recess duty. It's funny how your reaction to getting called by the principal is the same no matter how old you are: your sphincter clenches and you look for someone else to blame. I wasn't really in trouble, though. And even if I was in trouble, my punishment was to play more kickball. When I came back in, the teacher apologized for not telling me about that and told me to finish my lunch break. This time the lounge was empty and I found an orphaned bag of potato chips.

While the class was watching an episode of *Goosebumps*, a kid came up to me and told me his tooth was really loose. Before I could finish telling him to leave it alone he had a bloody tooth in his hand.

Morgan Elementary School
September 27, 28

I worked one-on-one with an autistic boy. It was a disaster. It's hard enough to get an autistic kid to listen to you when he likes you. This one hated me. Luckily the teacher didn't care for me either and the other two EAs tried to talk to me as little as possible, so it was a clean sweep.

I had to monitor the kid in the bathroom. He went into the stall, dropped his pants and started shitting and screaming.

"You need to be quiet in there."

"Call me Buzz Lightyear."

"What?"

"Call me Buzz Lightyear!"

"OK, keep quiet in there... Buzz Lightyear."

There was a pregnant pause, then he started screaming again. I didn't want to invade his privacy, but after ten minutes of this I had to open the stall door and tell him to wash his hands and get back to class.

I stayed with my one-on-one in the lunch line. There was a first grade class ahead of us, really little kids. A girl kissed a boy on the top of his head. Cute. Then another boy got out of line, came over and shouted, "She showed us her titties!" while pointing to the girl's chest. "Show us again!" Not so cute. He tried to pull her shirt down but she just pushed him away.

Murray Elementary School
October 2-9

I got called to work one-on-one with a boy who was paralyzed from the neck down for a week of half days. The previous EA just got a full time job and now this position was vacant. The student was awesome and super cheerful. It made me feel like a jerk for being so bummed out about money. I mostly helped him by putting his assignments in front of him. He had a metal stick about the size of a straw which he held in his mouth and used to type. Or I could put a pencil at the end of it and he could write or draw. The nurse who worked with him was really friendly, too. I was surprised how nice the other kids at the school were. During recess they always invited him to play.

On Wednesday I watched as the nurse put a little suction tube into the hole in his throat to vacuum up the phlegm. He couldn't cough. At recess I asked if he was cold, which was a faux pas as he couldn't feel anything below his neck.

Thursday went well. Even though he was in a class with other kids, it was really he and I off to the side doing one thing while they all did another. I never talked to the other kids. Before I left today a bunch of kids introduced themselves to me. A few asked if I would lift them up. Then a few asked if they could lift me up. Once you've given a kid the OK to try to lift you up, they won't stop until they've either lifted you or pulled your legs out from under you. Luckily I caught myself.

They called me back on Monday morning. They wanted me to fill this position permanently, but I was going to make this my last day here. Though I liked this job, I needed more hours. Early in the day I had my student read a book to me. " 'Eddie and Sparky are best friends.' Like me and you!" Then he asked if I was coming back tomorrow. I caved in. How could

I say no to my best friend? Plus, he had been going to another class for reading and that teacher decided she didn't want him in her class anymore. His home room teacher didn't know what to do with him. I was left in charge of his education. I didn't think it would be fair to leave him with someone new.

On Tuesday I asked if I could get an afternoon class or if they could use me in the office, anything to get more hours. It was no use. I was left in charge of my student all day again, having to make up assignments for him. The nurse was really helpful in telling me at what levels he could work and ways I could make assignments easier for him, but it was up to me to decide what to do and when.

Wednesday was my last day at Murray. My one-on-one was given a laptop computer today. He was excited and wanted to work on it all day. That made things easy for me, although I did have a little trouble getting him to work on his journal. He kept drawing silly pictures.

As I left, my student called out to me, "See you Monday!" I kind of stammered that he probably wouldn't. I felt really bad for leaving, but when I got outside and the rain poured in through the holes in my shoes and I didn't have enough money to buy lunch I realized I couldn't afford to live on half-day pay.

Knox High School
October 16-18

I worked one-on-one with a student in a wheelchair in the Life Skills room. The first day the class went on a field trip to Goodwill. The kids got a tour of the sorting and pricing area behind the store. I worked at different Goodwill for a couple months when I first moved here and I know how bad that place really is, how they totally exploit people with disabilities. They put their employees with developmental disabilities on their billboards and in their commercials, but at the store where I worked there was a guy who had been there almost 20 years and was still making only a dollar above minimum wage. I should have asked the woman giving the tour about that. I gritted my teeth through the whole "isn't Goodwill wonderful" spiel. At the conclusion of the tour we were "invited" to shop at the store. Aw, thanks! A student went to the book section and read to me. Then he kept hitting on a girl in the class, calling her baby and telling her he was going to buy her a present. It was getting weird. She was trying to ignore him. I didn't know how to handle the situation. The kids never said anything blatantly creepy, he just wasn't getting the hint. You can't yell at a kid for being clueless, can you? I tried to tell him to leave her alone, she didn't want to be bothered, but he wouldn't hear it.

Then I had to help my student in the restroom. I helped him out of his chair, braced him as he stood in front of the urinal, and pulled his pants down. When he was finished I had to pull his pants back up, get him back in his chair and strap him down.

The class met back up in front of Goodwill. Despite my asking him to stop, and trying to physically stop his chair, my student kept wheeling into the wet grass, leaving long, muddy, torn up streaks in Goodwill's lawn. On the way back to school my student ran over a dead bird. It was an accident; I don't think he even noticed. In class the teacher read a Harry Potter book to the class. I read *Alexander's Bridge*. Then the kids played a board game as part of a social skills developing assignment or something. As anyone who has met me knows, my social skills are *nonpareil*, so I opted out of the game and did a crossword instead.

My student went on another field trip the next day, this time with his mainstream art class. The rest of the class went on a school bus that wasn't wheelchair equipped, so we took a cab down to the museum. The driver was a real serious looking guy named Hawk. It was hard not to laugh when he started singing along to Bonnie Raitt. Let's give them something to talk about? OK, how about I'm in a cab being driven by a guy who has a black beret and a soul patch and, oh yeah, did I mention he has a metal hook for a left hand?

We only had an hour and a half at the museum, and most of that time was wasted listening to banal discussions about one piece of art instead of letting the kids look at as many works of art as they could. I tuned out and wandered around the room, looking at the Roy Lichtensteins. We didn't have enough time to check out the European Masters. Instead we made a not as quick as I'd've hoped trip to the bathroom and then back to the cab. Hawk took us to a private catholic university.

Upon our arrival I asked my student if he'd rather eat or go to the bathroom first. He said eat. We looked around for a table, which took us up two floors, and I pulled his lunch out of his backpack, unwrapped everything and spread it out before him. After two bites he decided he had to go to the bathroom. This may be a petty complaint, but when you've asked a student what he wants to do several times and he tells you one thing, then you spend ten minutes preparing that thing only to have him change his mind and now you have to put everything back, knowing you'll have to take it all out again in ten minutes, it's frustrating.

After eating we went on a tour of the art spaces on campus. My patience was worn thin as my one-on-one didn't pay any attention to the art, opting instead to leer at girls. I know that's what high school boys do, but come on, a little subtlety wouldn't kill you. Again I politely asked him to leave the girls alone so they could look at the prints; again I went unheeded. He wheeled around the room (he didn't have a firm grasp on how large his chair was and he nearly ran into people several times) trying to get close to any group of girls. With other students you can pull them back or get in their way, but I felt powerless against a motorized wheelchair. Plus my student repeatedly told me he was going to put the smack down on me, which didn't add to my patience. The final straw came when we were checking out the larger pieces outside. One of the pieces was a crooked little shed with gravel inside. It was more artistic than I make it sound. Students were told to walk through it to get a feel for it. I asked him not to try. He immediately went for it, bumping into people on his way. And, as I feared, he got stuck in the gravel. I needed the art teacher's help in getting him out. I tried as hard as I could not to snap at him the rest of the day, which isn't easy when I have to explain over and over again that if you only have $1.21, you can't get a $1.25 cola from a vending machine.

We got out at 1:59 and waited for the cab that was supposed to be there at 2:00. I had to tell the student at least 15 times, maybe 20, that I wasn't going to call the driver on his cell phone to remind him to pick us up by the time the cab arrived at 2:02.

I think I reached the pinnacle of my frustration during art on Thursday. The class was watching a boring video on etching. My student told me he had to go to the bathroom. To get to the bathroom from the art class, I had to take him through the storage room and woodshop, through three locked doors and up a service elevator. When we got to the bathroom I had to get him out of his chair and pull his pants down. He stood there for maybe two seconds and said, "I'm done." He obviously didn't do anything and was just trying to get out of class. I called him on it, but he wouldn't say anything. I don't understand how a 15-year-old kid wouldn't have a problem with a stranger pulling down his pants just to get out of watching a video.

DuBois Middle School
October 22

I was going to refuse this assignment because middle schools are bad in general and I had a bad experience at DuBois in particular, but I accepted when I was told it was the Life Skills class. When I got to work I realized it was not the Life Skills room at all, but the A-room. It went well, though. For math I worked with two kids doing money stuff. They were really into it and turned it into a game. To the teacher, it must have looked like I was doing a great job, but really the kids were doing everything.

At the end of the day I took a group of 5 students and had them each choose three words from a list to define. Some kids were giggling and I knew they were looking up dirty words in the dictionary, but I make it a rule not to get mad at students for doing something I might have done (or still do).

Cleese Elementary School
October 24

This class had seven really low functioning first and second graders. There were four adults in the room and sometimes that wasn't enough. The day was that rough.

It started out harmless enough. I had to walk with a kid as he carried the breakfast tray back to the cafeteria. Every four or five steps he'd stop, set the tray down, and lie on the floor. I'd tell him to get up and he'd take four or five more steps then lie down again. This happened all the way down the hall and all the way back. He wasn't trying to be difficult, it was just something he did. And every time I asked him to get up, he seemed like he wanted to say something like, "Oh yeah! I forgot, I shouldn't be on the floor. Oops!"

Things soon got worse. One of the kids was autistic. He couldn't speak, but he did moan all day. He'd lick his hand and grab me. I sat next to him at circle time. The teacher interrupted reading the story to warn me that that kid likes glasses. I turned around in just in time to see him grabbing at mine. I moved fast enough to avoid him grabbing my glasses, but not fast enough to avoid a slobbery thumb in my eye. A little later, still during circle, he turned to me and started screaming. It's really unnerving to see a kid with a blank expression screaming uncontrollably. Upon hearing this, the kid sitting on my other side burst into tears and started hitting himself in the head. I don't mean little pats, I mean full on punches to his head. I reached across his body to grab his arm and he bit me. By then another kid was crying and a fourth was running around the room. This was the most helpless and awful I've ever felt in a classroom.

After lunch the kids had choosing. I had to man the bean table, which was, as the name implies, a table full of beans for kids to run their hands through. It was a tactile thing for the autistic kids. There was one kid at my station and my job was to make sure she didn't eat any beans. I failed. I held my hand under her mouth and told her to spit the bean out. A big foamy glob of spit fell into my hand, but no bean. I washed my hand and counted down the seconds until school was out. I felt guilty for being so useless and I wanted to apologize to the teacher.

There was one good part of the day, though. During circle time, before the explosion, as I was sitting next to the autistic boy, I crossed my legs. He immediately threw a leg over mine. If you've ever watched a Marx Brothers movie, you know how funny that can be. Other than that, had this been my first day I probably would have quit.

Crane Elementary School
October 30

I missed my stop on the bus and had to walk 15 blocks in the pouring rain down streets with no sidewalks. I was splashed by cars several times before I finally reached the school.

I worked in the Life Skills with Nursing class, the lowest functioning kids in the district. These were nonverbal kids with no motor control. Most had feeding tubes although a couple could be spoon fed, but only if their meal was puréed. These kids didn't even do basic things like look at someone who was talking to them or follow people or toys with their eyes.

The first project of the day was making paper bag pumpkins. Each staff would grab a students hand and hold a paintbrush to it, then make the student paint the bag. While doing this, some of the students were having mild seizures, tensing up and gurgling. It was depressing. Then I folded laundry. You'd be surprised how many towels a class of 8 kids can go through in a day. Then we played bingo. The teacher would read off a number and we'd put the student's card in front of their face. If they had it, we'd get all excited, put a dry erase pen in the student's hand and help them mark the square. If they didn't have it we'd get really dramatic and say, "Oh, no! You don't have that one. Maybe the next one!" Some of the kids were asleep when we did this. It's hard to muster any enthusiasm when the kids aren't even conscious.

Then the kids went home. But they didn't really go home. Since they're medically fragile, they live at the hospital. When I walked back to the bus, the rain and the lack of sidewalks didn't seem so bad anymore.

Harrison High School
October 31

I tried to get an elementary school assignment for Halloween, but I got sent to a high school. I worked one-on-one with a kid with Downs Syndrome. One of my jobs was to stop him from rocking back and forth and humming by grabbing his shoulder and speaking in a calm, soothing tone. I helped him make a jack-o-lantern: I carved the face and he scooped the guts. He was very thorough. The last two hours of the day was a party for Halloween and a student's 16th birthday. There wasn't anything to do, so I did what I always do when I get bored: I went through the desk of the guy I was subbing for. I just found a packet of bus tickets when the teacher told me to go home. I got paranoid that he thought I was stealing stuff from the EA's desk, but really he was just being nice and letting me go early.

Barrymore Elementary School
November 1, 2

As I got to school a girl asked me if I was a student. I said I was, but as it turns out she was in my class so I had to fess up. I worked one-on-one with an autistic kid. Mostly I repeated directions to him and helped him stay focussed. During lunch a kid said, "You look funny." Another kid called me Mr. Funnyglasses.

On Friday my student said he had to look in the mirror. I told him he could look later but he kept insisting. I thought it was just his autism causing him to get distracted, but when he sat next to me I noticed his ear was bleeding.

Polk High School
November 14, 19

This was a behavior room. First block I led a reading lesson, then had kids work in their workbooks. Some kid grabbed the workbook of a student who had finished and started copying the answers. I pulled the workbook away. He asked me why I was trying to act hard. I said I wasn't, I just wasn't going to let him cheat. He threatened to "bomb on" me. Two kids started wrestling second block and knocked a chair into my shin. Everyone showed up late to third block. A student went to the bathroom and came back missing his shoes. He said some kids, kids who didn't even go to Polk, just took them and ran off. Everyone bolted out of the classroom. Most kids came back right away, but a small contingent were gone for a while. Eventually they came back with the shoes.

Crane Elementary School
November 20

This was the Life Skills with Nursing class in which I had previously subbed. We did a project that involved crumpling paper to make it look like corn husks, then gluing dyed corn kernels onto it. The student I was working with was asleep, so I did the whole thing by myself and set the finished product on his chest.

Before school ended, a girl grabbed my hand and held it against her face. It may not sound like much, but it was an emotional display for a kid who couldn't talk.

Morgan Elementary School
November 29

I went to a Life Skills class in which I had subbed before, the one with the autistic kid who didn't like me and the staff that didn't talk to me. It was awkward. Last time I subbed here I was supposed to work for a week and a half, but I asked my boss to send me somewhere else after two days. So now the teacher and EAs knew I didn't want to be there; that didn't make them want to talk to me any more.

They had me work one-on-one with the toughest kid in the class. Nothing could hold his attention for more than a couple seconds. I put a letter tracing worksheet in front of him and he threw a fit. First he tried to grab the box of worksheets away from me. When I wouldn't let him, he threw a pencil and crawled under the table and pretended to cry.

In the lunch line I told the kids in other classes I was a new fourth grade student. They didn't believe me.

DiMarco Elementary School
December 4, 5

I worked in the kindergarten class. The morning class went well. At recess I pulled kids in a wagon, going faster and faster until one of them fell out. During free time I manned a marble trail made of Duplo blocks. My job was to fix it when kids broke it, which happened at intervals of no more than 25 seconds. When the teacher told them to free time was over they broke the whole thing before I could stop them. I mean they took their fists to it and destroyed it in under five seconds. I had to rebuild it in the break between the a.m. and p.m. classes. I was kind of upset that it cut into my 45 minute lunch break, but then I realized I was getting paid to play with Duplo blocks.

The next day I got to class before anyone else, so I helped myself to some of the snack time raisins. The a.m. class went the same as yesterday, except I didn't pitch any kids from the wagon at recess.

I was only supposed to go for a half a day, but half way through my lunch at a nearby cafe the other EA tracked me down to ask me to come back for the p.m. class. I was looking forward to having the day off, but it was worth going back when all the kids seemed excited to see me. The friend I had to break plans with probably wouldn't have given me such a warm welcome. One kid said he wished the woman I was subbing for would be sick tomorrow so I could come back. That's nice, right?

There was an intruder drill an hour into class. The teacher shut out the lights and put a piece of paper over the window in the door and the kids had to sit against the wall as quietly as possible. We passed out crackers and peanut butter as an incentive to stay quiet. I found out the school has the same procedure in case of a wild animal.

Robertson Elementary School
December 6

I got to work a little late. This was a fourth and fifth grade behavior room. The kids introduced themselves to me and I thought the day wouldn't be so bad. They asked me if I dyed my hair black. They didn't believe me when I said that was my natural color, pointing to my reddish brown sideburns as proof I was lying. How do you argue with that?

Early on a couple kids asked if they could run laps outside to burn off some excess energy. The other EA and I took them out. They didn't run much, so I raced them. This marked the last moment of enjoyment I'd have until I got home. The other EA got called to another class, so it was just me and those two kids outside. They went crazy. They refused to go in and tried to slam the door on my fingers to lock us out. Eventually they went back to class, but it was accompanied by a lot of running, pounding on the walls and lots of profanity. The teacher asked me to escort them to the bathroom. I said I'd only do it one at a time, but they both ran out before I could finish speaking. They both had to defecate and sat in neighboring stalls. One kid threw his soiled clod of toilet paper over the partition into his friend's stall.

Things calmed down a little after that. I helped those same two boys with a map/state name anagram assignment and they really got into it. They even worked on it through their break time.

The teacher left me alone with the kids as they ate their lunch in the classroom. Of course things went badly. I put on a claymation Christmas video, but only two kids were interested. Two kids who out-weighed me by quite a bit chased each other around the room. The high point of lunch was when a girl told me she didn't eat meat. I told her I was a vegetarian, too. "Actually, I'm what's called a vegan." I explained what that meant and why I do it (all at her prompting, I never force kids to listen to my propaganda) and she really mulled it over. One more soldier for the Vegan Holy War.

Later a kid started acting up, bumping into kids and acting unsafe. The teacher cleared all the other students out of the room. The other EA and I stayed in the room with the kid. I guess a room clear is a pretty serious offense, because he got really upset and threw his water bottle across the room. He tried to leave to join the rest of the class but the other EA stopped him. The kid totally freaked out. He was bawling his eyes out and screaming and cursing. The other EA had to restrain him bodily. I stuck around to see if I needed to call the principal or the kid's mom or something. In the middle of the kid's tantrum he stopped crying and calmly asked if he hit me when he threw the water bottle. I told him I got splashed. He apologized, then went back to screaming and kicking. It was hard to watch and I felt ridiculous just standing there, not being able to do anything. Eventually the other EA took him to the office and the rest of the class came back.

I was asked to help a girl with her math assignment. She narrowed her eyes and quietly, but with a great deal of animosity, told me to get away. The teacher got mad at me when I backed away and told me to help the girl. I tried again. This time the girl said she hated me before telling me to go away.

Morgan Elementary School
December 7

This was the Life Skills with Nursing class I'd been in many times before. Our first project was working hand-over-hand with students to crumple brown paper to look like antlers. We taped those to the headrests of the wheelchairs so when the kids leaned back it looked like they had antlers, kind of. We also crumpled red paper into balls and taped them to the kids' noses. Then we lined the kids up and took a picture. One kid was asleep on a mat, so I sat in her chair for the picture.

Thurston Elementary School
December 10-14

This class was awesome. The class introduced themselves to me and the teacher just had me kind of lurk around and watch how the class went. Then I worked with two kids on math. I gave them piles of coins and they had to tell me how much it was worth. They got really into it and turned it into a game. Luckily math ended as the game started to get out of hand. As I put the change away I told a kid I was cold. His response was, "If you got some muscles you'd be ok." But he didn't say it in a mean way, it was like he was looking out for me. During lunch he asked me if I had any friends. Again, it wasn't supposed to be an insult.

The next day I got to work early and availed myself of the coffee in the office. It was hot and very nearly mediocre. I went with a kid to his mainstream class in the library and took notes on how he did. I turned my notes in to the teacher after class. Then the kid confessed he had threatened another student. I hadn't heard that. I felt kind of dumb, I was given one job and I blew it.

A boy refused to do his work, then kind of flipped out. He just rolled around on the floor. No kicking, no screaming, no profanity, and no shit-stained projectiles... sounds good to me. The teacher and the other EA stayed behind to deal with this kid as I took the rest of the class to an assembly on Native American ceremonial dances,

On Wednesday one of the kids threw up on the bus and I had to walk with him out to his grandmother's car so he could go home. She asked me if I thought it was the meds or if he was sick. I said I thought he threw up because I gave him $5 to eat a pile of chinchilla shit. No, I didn't. I just shrugged.

Every morning the class would check in with the teacher. They

talked about how they felt and what their goal for the day was. On Friday one of the kids decided to have me check in. I said I was sad because it was my last day working here. I got a lot of "Aaaw!"s, but not nearly as many as I got when I said my goal was to try not to burst into tears at the end of the day.

We went on a field trip to the library for the last couple hours of the day. Luckily it was a small library so the kids couldn't run off too far. One student came up to me and told me a couple other kids were looking at sex books. I walked down the aisles and came to two kids hurriedly reshelving a book with a pregnant woman on the cover. I didn't want to bust them because I know I might have done something similar at that age (although I don't think a book on how to keep healthy during pregnancy would have been my first choice.) I just acted like I was looking for a book in that aisle, figuring they'd move along. I flipped open a book on apes. I felt embarrassed and like a hypocrite when I came across a picture of Bonobos humping, although I did learn that Bonobos are one of the only other animals to practice face-to-face intercourse.

The rest of the time in the library went without incident, unless you consider a pudgy kid saying, "Look! *Reptiles for Dummies*!" loudly to no one in particular an incident. We checked out our books and headed over to a coffeeshop for hot chocolate. I got coffee (Ms. R, if you're reading this, I don't think I thanked you for the coffee. Thank you, that was very nice. And M.K., I'm sorry for leaving my coffee cup on your desk when I left.) The pudgy kid of *Reptiles for Dummies* fame blew the top off his hot chocolate cup, spilling some on the table, which caused him to let out the shrillest scream I've ever heard in my life.

Back in class, the kids all said goodbye and thanked me, at the other EA's prompting. "No, thank *you*!" I said. We went back and forth thanking each other until finally I said, "OK, you're welcome." A boy said, "No, *you're* welcome!" I walked the kids out to the bus and took off. On my way out I saw a kid peeing on the school. He had the audacity to scowl at me for laughing.

Student Services Building
December 20

The Student Services Building is a three story brick building, most of it offices for school administrative purposes, but there were a few classes on the third floor. I was under the impression that SSB was for younger kids (judging from the playground) with emotional problems. I was wrong. I got there as the students were going to lunch. They were high school students. I asked the teacher why they were here instead of other schools. They all got kicked out of their other schools. "The worst of the worst" is how he put it. The teacher wanted me to go by my last name, but when I told him it was Roche, he had the class call me Mr. R. The kids came back from lunch and the snickering began. One girl walked in, laughed at me and had to leave the room to compose herself.

My first job today was to escort two students to the bathroom. My directions were simple: I was to let one kid in at a time, poking my head in and checking for smoke before and after each student. Yeah, I was paid to sniff a high school bathroom.

I tried to help a girl use the internet to look up one of her relatives. I found the white pages for the city she asked for, but I couldn't find the person she was looking for. I felt kind of bad for not being much help. The teacher took me aside and told me it was for the best I didn't come up with anything. She was looking for her father who she hadn't had any contact with in three years. Now I felt sad and useless.

The last two periods of the day were computer classes. I helped set up laptops and occasionally asked kids to stop looking for naked pictures of Britney Spears.

Transition Class
January 7, 8

I had to take a student to the bathroom. Luckily, all I had to do there was take off his fanny pack and put it back on him when he was done, but I had to stick around the bathroom to make sure things went ok. It was awkward. Do I talk to him in there? Do I look at him while I talk to him? I pretended to fix my hair and said something that didn't necessarily need to be answered.

For the last hour of the day the class watched an excruciatingly boring video on Rumi. I had to ask two students to stop talking and even threatened to separate them. I hate doing stuff like that.

When my student got to class on the second day I put him in a stander. That's a vertical wooden thing on wheels to which the student is strapped. It's not as bad as it sounds. It's to help strengthen the legs.

A few students ate lunch in the classroom and I talked with them over my crossword. I mentioned that I lived in Los Angeles. One kid asked me, "How are the hookers in L.A.?" I thought maybe I had misheard him but he continued, "I've only been there five times, but you lived there so you would know better." I said I didn't know how to answer that and changed the subject.

Besser Elementary School
January 10, 11

I worked one-on-one with a girl with Down's Syndrome. Her class was outside when I arrived, which was well over an hour late. Her mother was there subbing for me until I showed up. It's really nerve-wracking to work with a difficult kid while her mother is watching. I wanted to look like I knew what I was doing, but I didn't want to be too forceful. My solution: let her mother do everything until she leaves. The kid seemed to be ok with her mother leaving, but as soon as she was out of sight my troubles began. Trying to get her out of the library turned out to be an ordeal. She fell to the floor, and after failing to coax her into standing I'd pick her up. I'd get to take two or three steps and she'd fall to the floor again. It was like a silent comedy, except it was kind of loud. And it wasn't funny.

She was in a mainstream class, but, as she was nonverbal, she really oughtn't have been. It didn't seem fair to her to be put in a class where she couldn't possibly do even half the work the rest of the class was doing, and it didn't seem fair to the class to have a girl that needed a lot of individual attention. I mean, there's something to be said for mainstreaming special ed. students, but this wasn't an ideal situation. The teacher wasn't fond of the set up, either. Her solution was to keep her and the class totally separate; she would run the class per usual and the EA would be in charge of the girl's education. As such, the teacher didn't give me any help, and I very clearly needed it. The usual EA left me notes telling me loosely what her schedule should be, but it kept referring to the student's materials being in tubs and I couldn't find those tubs until halfway through the day. To be fair, it's not like the tubs were hidden, but when you're working with a kid that has to be closely watched all the time, you can't wander around the room looking for something. The sub notes also said to take her to the corner of the room and read to her if things weren't going well. I spent at least three-quarters of the day there.

I took her to the bathroom before lunch. Her diaper was wet. I tried to change it but she kept squirming around and trying to run away from me. I wasn't comfortable with the situation at all so I asked the teacher for help. She changed the diaper while I held the girl still.

The second day went pretty much the same, except the girl was flatulent. I don't know how the rest of the class kept from laughing. I had a hard time. I guess today's second graders are just more mature than me. I went through every Dr. Seuss and P.D. Eastman book in the reading corner. I had a surprisingly easy time changing her diaper by myself, and the fire drill went well.

Urban Education Center
January 15

UEC is a K-12 alternative school. The students there are really independent and self-motivated. I worked one-on-one with a girl with physical disabilities. I didn't have much to do as she got around pretty well by herself and, like any other 10-year-old girl, didn't want to ask a stranger for help.

I went to lunch with my student. There were some punk kids there, one with a Minor Threat shirt and the other with Crass patches. I was going to whistle a Minor Threat song as I walked by, but realized it's impossible to whistle Minor Threat songs. Only later did it occur to me how horribly geeky it would have been to whistle a song just to prove to the kids I've got cred. Why don't I just whip out the ticket stub from the first time I saw Fugazi? That'd be cool, right?

I really didn't do anything the rest of the day. The class watched two film strips, then worked on a group project. I just wandered around the room. At the end of the day the girl's mother came to pick her up. It was the woman who does Food Not Bombs on Thursdays. I asked her not to tell anyone that I'm secretly a punk and a freeloader.

Polk High School
January 28

This was a transition class for 18- to 21-year-old kids. We went on a field trip to a shopping mall in the suburbs. If you ever see me at a mall in ths suburbs, rest assured I'm getting paid for it. I was asked to follow one student, as she had a tendency to wander around and get lost. I tried not to be too obvious about it, but it's hard for me to look inconspicuous in a shop aimed at adolescent girls. I just can't act like I'm genuinely interested in glittery fingernail polish.

Urban Education Center
February 7

I worked one-on-one with a middle school student. I felt like there was no reason for me to be there, as she didn't seem to need any special attention.

The last class of the day was spent in the library, supposedly researching. I helped my student find stuff on space exploration. I realized none of the other kids were really working, so after setting her up with some books, I gave her some space so she could goof off, too. Then I figured I might as well not work either, so I took out my journal and wrote. Oh, yeah, there was a girl wearing a shirt with a picture of the Sex Pistols and "Punk Rock" written in spangles.

Besser Elementary School
February 8

I worked one-on-one with a mildly autistic student. He kept getting distracted during math. I threatened to draw a beard and moustache on him with a ballpoint pen if he didn't get to work. It backfired. He wanted me to draw facial hair on him. When I wouldn't he grabbed a red crayon and tried to color his face.

During free time most of the kids wanted to play with me. I played Ice Breaker, Candyland (twice), and helped with brontosaurus and magnetic alphabet puzzles. Also, many Lego planes and cars were brought to me for my approval.

At the end of the day a girl's mother came in and handed out invitations to a Valentine's Day Party. The girl asked if I could come to the party. I could sense her mother tensing up, so I politely declined.

Clouster Elementary School
February 12

I got called to work late and subsequently got to school late, right in the middle of the first break for free time. I played chess with a kid and he beat me. I didn't let him win.

Towards the end of the day I kind of worked one-on-one with a kid. He was rebellious but for some reason he worked well with me. I took him to the Reading Cafe, a classroom with nice chairs, a radio, and tons of books. He sat in a rocking chair and read a book on cars. I lied on a bean-bag chair and read a book about Louis Braille. With 45 minutes left of school we joined the class to watch a video on the planets. The other EA snickered and made a puerile comment when the part on Uranus came up. One of the students said it wasn't funny. The EA snapped back, "You don't get it." The kid said he got it, it just wasn't funny. That made me very happy.

February 14

I got called to Taft High School for a half day. I was told to show up at 11:10 and to dress comfortably. I've never been called to a class where it was specified to dress comfortably. Did this class have a problem with subs showing up in girdles or Zoot suits or something? I was debating whether a tube top or a mesh jersey would be more comfortable when I got another call. My boss told me not to go to Taft, they needed someone with more specialized skill, I'm guessing maybe some medical background. If I had just let that call go to the machine I could have slept in, gone to Taft, acted like I didn't know I wasn't supposed to come in, been sent home right away and collected four hours pay. As it was I just got to sleep in for free.

Taft High School
February 19

I got sent to the Life Skills class in which I subbed for a month and a half at the end of last year. The teacher was really glad to see me. Early on she berated a student for having dirty hair and made her wash it in the sink in the storage room behind the classroom. I wondered how glad the teacher would be to see me if she knew that not only did I not shower that morning, but I was wearing the same clothes I wore to a show last night. I stayed on the opposite side of the room so she couldn't smell me.

The class took a walking field trip to a nearby supermarket. The teacher asked me if I was still writing. I said I was. She asked what I was writing. I didn't know what to say, so I lied. I told her I was submitting stuff to magazines. She said that was something she wanted to get into and asked me how to go about it. I tried to remain as vague as possible, say-ing it depended on which magazines you were submitting stuff to. She said she wanted to send stuff to Christian magazines, specifically Billy Graham's. Yikes! You're really asking the wrong guy. I wanted to say, "Well, usually you have to sleep your way in," but decided that wasn't funny enough to warrant all the trouble I'd bring on myself.

Robertson Elementary School
February 20

As I got to work (late, of course) I realized this was the school where I had one of the worst experiences of my life; the school in which the kid threw his used toilet paper at his friend. I was hoping I'd be in a different class, but luck wasn't with me. Within seconds of stepping into the classroom a kid angrily asked me why I was there. I was tense all day, waiting for a kid to explode like last time. It didn't happen, but the day was still awful. I was told to go home, called a dork, and asked, "What are you staring at, freak?" I've never been around a group of kids so devoid of charm. Whereas the kids hated me, the teacher just ignored me, not giving me a chance to take any breaks, not even for lunch.

Before the day ended the teacher and I took the class outside. We stood next to each other while the kids played basketball. A silence so palpable and profound it almost had an odor hung between us. After school the teacher asked me to sweep the classroom. Fuck you.

Peirmont Elementary School
February 22

The secretary told me the behavior problem class I was working in was in the only portable classroom. Then she walked me to it, as if I might get lost finding the one portable in the schoolyard.

The teacher was really nice. He gave me a detailed outline of what we were going to do and what was expected of me before school started. It might not sound like much, but it's rare for a teacher to do that and it's so helpful. The first kid in the class told me he liked my shirt. This day was off to a good start. Although some of the students, especially one girl, were a little sassy, my day stayed good. I had a little trouble during word bingo, though. I made the mistake of giving kids little multicolored bears to mark their cards instead of bingo chips. The kids would much rather arranged the bears by color than win some dumb word game. By the third game I had to take away the bears and give them chips. They were upset with me for that, but I won them back at recess.

It was obvious these kids weren't used to adults playing around or swinging on the monkey bars. A kid from another class asked me who I was. I pointed to one of my African-American students and said I was his father. We both thought that was pretty funny.

I monitored the kids at lunch. I pulled the "Oh, what did you get me" while reaching for their food trick way too many times, but it always got a laugh.

The last hour or so of the day was a birthday party. The class drew cards for the birthday boy. A kid got frustrated because he thought he couldn't draw. He kept crumpling up his papers and throwing them away, getting madder each time. I helped him out by showing him I draw badly, but I don't care. He and the kid next to him liked my drawing of the birthday boy, probably because I gave him vampire fangs and a stovepipe hat. My tactic backfired when they got in an argument over who could keep my picture.

After juice and cookies, there was another short recess. I chased kids around and banged me knee on the slide. I pretended to fall asleep so the kids wouldn't see me limping.

Kennedy High School
February 25, 26

After lunch, the two special ed. classes got together to clean the cafeteria. I don't know if this happens everywhere, but at every high school here they have the lower functioning special ed. kids wash the dishes and wipe down the tables. It's supposed to be a job skills class: students learn to obey orders, work well with others, etc., but it seems messed up to me to take away from class time to make the kids do janitorial work for the school for free (although they do get a cookie when they're done). But the kids don't complain so maybe I shouldn't either.

The next day there was an assembly on prejudice. Some white guy with facial tattoos and tons of piercings talked about how he's discriminated against and how he learned that's wrong. He legally changed his name to Scary Guy. It was really stupid.

I went back to the class after the assembly to find there was a sub for the teacher, too. She was kind of crazy. She thought I was a student, even though I had worked with her at another school before. She would go off on weird tangents while lecturing to the students, mostly about how her father was a house painter. He was good and he worked cheap because he got paid under the table. She also spent half an hour of class time making phone calls to try to get a refund on the sixty-five cents she lost in the vending machine.

Kennedy High School
March 5

My class went on a field trip to the ballet. I was asked to stay behind with the few kids who didn't get their permission slips signed or just didn't want to go. There were two kids in second period. I gave them math worksheets and sat with them and wrote a letter. One of the kids asked me if I had ever had a girlfriend. He wasn't trying to be mean, he seemed concerned for me. He even gave me advice: if I wore smaller glasses and baggier clothes, I'd get more girls. He asked if I had a cd player or a stereo. I asked if he thought that after work I went home and sat alone in an empty, silent room. Then he asked if I like big boobs. I said I wasn't going to answer anymore questions and went back to my letter. I ignored him when he asked if I went to strip bars. Then he told me he sometimes watches pornos with his dad. What?

Burton Elementary School
March 6

I was sent to Cleese Elementary school. I got there right on time, but there was a mistake. The woman I was supposed to sub for was there. She needed a sub tomorrow, not today. I was hoping they'd just send me home, but instead I was sent to Burton, the nearest school that needed a sub. I got back on the bus, then walked around in the rain lost for 20 minutes. By the time I got to work I was soaked.

I worked in a room with six autistic third to fifth graders. My first job of the day was to help out with deep relaxation. I had to massage kids. I really don't like starting my day with a highball of ridiculous and creepy. Though I have a lot of respect for the other EA and the teacher, the day massaging a 10-year-old kid's temples doesn't seem weird to me, the day it becomes a commonplace occurrence eliciting no more reaction than does changing a light bulb or checking my answering machine is verily the day I bite a cyanide capsule. I was supposed to massage another student, but she kicked at me so I called it quits. Another kid was acting up and thus didn't get his massage. Afterwards he begged for a massage and pleaded for forgiveness. He said, "I don't deserve your kindness!" at least five times.

Keida Elementary School
March 8

 There was an assembly on dental hygiene first thing in the morning. There was a green tooth, a brown tooth, and a yellow tooth. They all wanted to be white teeth. I got a toothbrush and floss out of the deal.

 After the assembly I took a few students from my first through third grade class to a mainstream music class. The kids were divided into four sections. One group played little bongo drums, another played xylophones, a third played maracas, and the fourth quizzed each other with flashcards of eighth, quarter, half, and whole notes. I wandered around the room playing the instruments with the kids. After half an hour, those kids left and another class came in. I got to sit in on three classes. Not to brag, but by the time the third class was over I had almost mastered the maracas.

The class got a little rambunctious when we went to the library. I slipped and told a girl to shut up when she called another kid a crybaby. She had been really obnoxious and rude all day and I just got frustrated. That was the first (and to this point only) time I blew up like that on a kid, and I've been spat on, yelled at, threatened, laughed at, ignored, and kicked in the nuts.

Tyler High School
March 11, 12

This was a behavior room. I didn't do much, mostly because the kids didn't do much so there was nothing for me to help with. The teacher told me to just hang out in the back of the class and I did. I barely even spoke and yet somehow the students took a liking to me, even telling me personal things about themselves. Third period the class went to PE. The teacher took off to make copies. I sat at my desk reading. Two girls came in and asked if they could play Uno. I didn't see why not. The had an in-depth discussion on pain killers. It was unnerving how much they knew about the various kinds and their side effects.

The second day was so easy it was ridiculous. It was a block schedule day. Two of the blocks were prep periods, which means there weren't any students. Plus school got out early. There was less than three hours of class time with students, and twenty minutes of that was silent reading. I was hoping I could sneak off the same time the students got out, but I had to stay until 3:00. That's ok, though, I finished Paul Robeson's *Here I Stand*.

Those precious few minutes I spent with students went well. They seemed glad to see me. I was greeted with "Big Dave's here!" There was lots of profanity throughout the day, but not aimed at anybody or anything. It was like they had to say something to make sure they were exhaling and "fuck" is as good a word as any.

Shore Elementary School
March 13, 14

This was a pre-kindergarten class for kids with autism. I mainly worked with one kid. I had to make sure he didn't run away and remind him to check his schedule. Almost all the kids with more severe autism that

I've worked with have schedules. It's just a line of velcro with little pictures of the days activities (story time, free time, circle, snack, art) stuck on in chronological order. After each activity the student removes that square and checks what's next. I used little plasic cars to bribe my student to check his schedule.

During free time a girl came up and handed me a bunch of foam letters, the kind that interlock. I stacked them on her head. She loved it.

At the end of the day the speech pathologist came in and had the kids circle around her. She had a list of ten words and, one by one, went around the circle and had the kids say them. I was in charge of keeping track of two students' speech, giving them a plus for each word they said right and a minus for each they got wrong. They were given a candy which they were to chew on one side of their mouth, then switch to the other side. I had to grade them on that as well.

Crane Elementary School
March 19

I got called in to the Life Skills with Nursing class, the lowest functioning kids in the district. I never know what to do in these classes. The kids don't respond when I try to interact with them and I'm not certified to do any of the important things (like feed students). I end up washing dishes and wiping down mats and toys.

It was the speech pathologist's birthday and the other two EAs made a cake for him, kind of. They took every edible item they could find (flour, peanut butter, and Pepto Bismal) and mixed it together to make a frosting of sorts. Then they spread this frosting over a coffee can to make it look like a cake. Unfortunately, they only had enough frosting to cover the top of the can, so it didn't really look like a cake. Instead, it looked like somebody whose diet consisted of silly putty and gazpacho shat on a coffee can.

DuBois Middle School
March 20-22

I got sent to do data entry at DuBois from 9 to 5 for three days. I was working in the detention room entering paper detention slips, referrals, suspensions, and expulsions in the new computer database. I felt like a jerk. All my life "this is going on your permanent record" has been a stupid, idle threat, and now here I am, making permanent records. What happened to me?

The job was pretty boring. I tried to keep myself entertained by reading the descriptions of the incidents that cause the suspension, detention, or referral, but they were all pretty prosaic: fighting, profane language, back talk. The best one I saw was two kid who got written up for arguing over who could fart louder. That's the problem with kids today, it's all about volume. When I was their age, it was about timing. Now that takes some finesse.

I decided to help myself to a 45 minute lunch break, thinking I was pulling a fast one. Later I learned that I was supposed to take an hour for lunch, so really I cheated myself out of 15 minutes.

I made a mistake and put the wrong day down for a student's detention. When I went back to fix it, I accidentally erased his whole record, a years worth of detentions and referrals gone. I decided not to tell anyone. You owe me, James.

By 4:30 school was long over and the other person in the detention room had taken off. Though there was no one to watch me, my strong work ethic compelled me to leave only 15 minutes early, not a half hour.

Freeman Middle School
April 4

During lunch one of my students made fun of me. Actually, he made fun of another student by saying he looked like me. Things are messed up when a kid uses you as the standard by which other geeks are measured.

Chavez Middle School
April 5, 8, 9

I subbed for the librarian. It was great. There wasn't very much for me to do, and what I was supposed to do I couldn't. Nobody knew the password to get into the computer. I couldn't even check out books the first half of the day. I'd just have the students sign their name, the name of the book, and the book's library number. I spent a lot of time reading *If on a Winter's Night a Traveler* and checking my e-mail. My biggest concern was finding a good time to leave the library to use the restroom. Eventually a student aide logged me into the computer and I had to type in all the books that had been checked out.

The student aide for the last period of the day was getting into punk rock. He had the names of his favorite bands written on his trapper keeper: Bad Religion, Green Day, Linkin Park, and Blink 182. Somehow They Might Be Giants and Hot Water Music ended up on there, too. He asked if he could play a cd on the computer. I asked if it was good music.

"It's Less Than Jake."

"That's ok. It's no Operation Ivy, but it'll do." He was excited I knew who Operation Ivy were. I bragged about some of the shows I went to. A girl who wasn't an aide but was hanging around asked if she could check out books to other students. I didn't see why not. I read while she did my job and the punk kid played with the demagnetizer.

I was called back on Monday and was asked to work there all week. It was a long bus ride to school but I was pleased to find out I was only 15 minutes late. Then I realized that the clocks hadn't been moved back for Daylights Saving and I was actually an hour and fifteen minutes late. Again, I didn't know how to log into the computer. The aide that helped me last time didn't show up today. I resorted to having the kids write their names and the books' titles and library numbers again. I was useless all day.

The neophyte punk kid came in and asked if he could play a Rancid cd on the computer. I let him. When it was over I put on Pinhead Gunpowder. I had my whole week planned. I was going to start with Pinhead Gunpowder, work my way through Dillinger 4, and by the end of the week get to Mohinder. My plans were ruined when I came in Tuesday morning. The principal told me the school couldn't afford to keep me for the rest of the week, there wasn't enough money in their budget for a substitute librarian. That seemed fair enough. It's not like I was doing anything that warranted getting paid. I just wonder who will step up and take over that kid's punk rock tutelage.

I finally found the codes and passwords to get into the computer on Tuesday, but I didn't let that get in the way of checking my e-mail and reading. Actually, I acted almost like a real librarian: I helped a kid look up books on Chinese art and I shelved books.

Polk High School
April 22, 23

This was a Life Skills class. There was a chubby kid who kept saying, "Excuse me?!?" in a near falsetto that was obnoxious. Another kid told him to "stop talking like a lady," which may be one of the funniest things I've ever heard.

First period was PE and I just stood around the weight room. In second period everyone talked about their weekend. I got to brag about how Joe and I moved a drum kit 80 blocks on our bikes. The class ate lunch in the classroom while watching "Mr. Rogers". Then it was off to clean the cafeteria.

The class was in the middle of a lesson on drugs and medicine when I got back from my lunch break. The teacher gave some scenario involving a drug or medicine and the kids would have to say whether it was legal, illegal, or legal with a prescription. Some examples: "You buy cold medicine." "Someone gives you codeine for a headache." "Someone tries to sell you crack."

Kennedy High School
April 26

First period was a class where students were taught how to make a budget, balance a checkbook, fill out a job application, how to handle yourself at an interview, etc. I helped a girl work out a monthly budget. I tried to tell her $200 a month on clothes was a little extravagant but she wasn't having it.

Later, I kicked a kid for making fun of my ears. Not hard, of course.

Polk High School
May 2

The teacher had spray painted something outside during lunch but brought it into the classroom before it had fully dried. The room stank of paint and had the students been forced to sit in the fumes for an hour and a half someone would have got sick. The teacher had to go to plan B: basketball for the entire class. We took the students down to the gym. I sat out, but the teacher and the other EA played 2-on-2 with a couple students. The teacher twisted his ankle and fell to the ground. A student laughed at him. I told him it wasn't funny. I felt guilty for lying.

I was in a different class the last period of the day. This period was sex education. Surprisingly, the kids weren't interested. They also didn't know what testes were. The teacher had to tell them testes were balls.

Taft High School
May 3

I had to find the janitor to unlock a door for me. I looked in the boiler room for him and got yelled at. I guess he thought I was one of those

67

deviant subs that likes to sneak into boiler rooms and shit in the corner. Or maybe he thought I was a student. I don't know. Either way he told me never to go in there again.

Crane Elementary School
May 6, 7

Of the four staff, three were subs today. First I sat with two kids while they ate breakfast: Doritos and gummy fruit candy. Then I took two kids to PE. They played tennis, kind of. They were trying to volley against the wall three times in a row. I nearly made a girl cry when I suggested that she shouldn't take two turns in a row.

Back in the classroom, one of the kids was getting so fidgety the teacher strapped him down to his chair. There was another kid who was pretty low functioning. He was new to the class and the teacher didn't know what to do with him yet, so he was also strapped down to his desk and left to play with toys all day.

Morgan Elementary School
May 13

I didn't really want to go to this class because I'd subbed here before and I remember the teacher and other EAs weren't particularly pleasant, at least not to me. I got to school a little late, but at the same time as one of the students. I walked him down to the cafeteria to join his classmates for breakfast. The other EA said hello to the student, looked at me and said nothing. I said hello and she looked away. Great. 25,200 seconds left. Tick tock.

I took an autistic kid to the gym after breakfast. He sat on a scooter board and held one end of a jump rope. I took the other end and pulled him around the gym. After a while I got tired and said, "OK, my turn" and surprisingly he agreed. I got on the board and he pulled me around.

I watched the kids at recess. I talked to one boy about pets. I asked if he wanted a pet monkey and he said no. I don't understand.

Transition Class
May 14 - 16

I had to "travel train" a student on my first day. My job was to get on the bus with him and make sure he knew when to pull the cord and when to get off the bus. He was going to his new job at a grocery store. I put my bike on the bus and went to the deep southeast part of town with him. I got off at his stop and rode my bike to an expensive private university nearby. The school year had just ended and the dumpsters were calling.

The next day I accompanied a student to the Industries for the Blind. It's a place that employs people who have developmental disorders in addition to blindness. My student's job there was to answer the phone and route the calls to the proper person. He only got five calls in the six hours we were there. We spent the down time reading a large print version of *Huckleberry Finn*.

I had to help him in the bathroom. While I was in the stall with him, pulling his pants and underwear down, another employee barged in and said proudly, "Look at my shirt!"

Next was lunch. I cut my student's hot dog into bite-size pieces. He finished eating with 15 minutes left in his lunch break. I took him out with me to look for something I could eat. I found a Chinese place. I only had one dollar on me, so I ordered steamed rice to go. The cashier said it was $2. I tried to pay with my debit card but they didn't accept them. I felt like a big deadbeat walking out of a place hungry because I couldn't afford a $2 bowl of rice. And my student saw the whole thing.

Back to work, which meant back to *Huckleberry Finn*. My student told me that he and the guy I was subbing for refer to me as "Punk Rock Dave." He asked if I had any propaganda. I said I'd bring some tomorrow if I got called back.

After work but before his cab picked him up, my student said he wanted to get rice from that Chinese Restaurant. Having embarrassed myself once there, I didn't particularly want to go back, but he talked me into it. The woman wouldn't get out of her chair until she saw the kid had a couple bills. He asked for steamed rice and she asked, "Do you want the $1 size or the $2 size?" What the fuck? Why wasn't I given that option? I wouldn't have looked like such a deadbeat in front of my student and I wouldn't have to worry that my name would change from "Punk Rock Dave" to "Can't Afford Rice Dave."

Lloyd Elementary School
May 22

This was a class for severely autistic children. There were 8 students and 9 staff. I worked one-on-one with a student for the first half of the day. I had to constantly watch him and keep him from running out of the class and to the nearest sink or fountain and playing with the water.

I worked with him in one of the six cubicles in the class. The cubicles were partly to keep the kids from getting distracted, but mostly so I could sit down and block the only exit my student had. The first thing we worked on was matching. I'd put a toothbrush and a plastic cow in front of him and hold up a toothbrush and ask him to hand me the one that was the same. I rewarded him by putting a hand-held massager against his chest or face. He loved it. Sometimes he would get candy, which was kept in a paper cup thumbtacked to the wall of the cubicle. When he got bored, which was frequent, he would thrash around. Twice he knocked everything off his desk and sent the cup of candy flying. That left me sitting in a chair, reaching to pick up candy and plastic farm animals with one hand and having my other hand ready to catch the kid when he decided to make a run for it.

He was being potty trained, so I had to take him to the restroom every 45 minutes or so. I had to open a locked file cabinet in the bathroom, put on rubber gloves, and pull out a special seat with a pee guard that fits over the toilet seat, all the while making sure he didn't run to the sinks. Of the five times I took him to the bathroom, he peed once and I changed his diaper once. The other three times I just stood there and tried to coax him into peeing.

The one time he peed in the toilet he was allowed to wash his hands in the sink as a reward. The other four times I had to get him off the toilet and get him to stand next to the file cabinet. I would open the file cabinet, then run to the stall to get the special seat. Both my hands were busy as I put the seat in a plastic bag, so I had to lift my leg to block him from running to the sink. He was staring at the sink, and I know had he tried to push my leg out of the way I probably wouldn't have been able to keep my balance and have enough strength in my leg to hold him back. It was a stressful day.

On my way to lunch a kid from another class asked me if I liked Mudvayne, or Spineshank, or one of those awful nouveau metal bands. I said no. "Linkin Park...?" He asked about a few more bands of that ilk and when I said no to all he said, "Humbug!" Humbug? Don't you need to have big sideburns á la Martin Van Buren and maybe a monocle before you can say "humbug?"

After lunch I worked with a different kid. He was a little higher functioning. I just had to focus his attention back on his art project when his mind started to wander. I took him to the gym for motor skills work.

He was belly down on a big swing. There were a few blocks by the swing. The physical therapist would tell him which color block and he'd swing by, pick it up, then swing to the other side and drop it in a box. A girl tried to get on the swing with him and he flipped out. He started flailing his arms, trying to punch anyone that came near him. I had a block thrown at me. Eventually he was taken back to class and put in time out.

The teacher read a story and I rewarded kids who paid attention with a cracker or a cheese puff. Then the kids went home. I thought they'd let me go after the students left, seeing as how I had just had a block thrown at my gut, but they asked me to stay fifteen more minutes so I could cut gummy bears in half with a plastic butter knife.

Cope-Grey Middle School
June 7

I got to work and realized I was in a middle school behavior problem room with two subs, and it was a couple days before the end of the school year. Things were not going to go well. We played bingo first period but the kids weren't so into it. They decided letting loose a constant stream of profanity while throwing bingo chips at each other was more fun.

Half the class went on a field trip and the eighth graders left for graduation practice, so there was only one student in third period. There was a Super Nintendo in the room and he and I played Super Mario 3 the whole period. He was really friendly with me while we were playing, but only while we were playing.

When the other students got back we had a party, as it was the last Friday of the year. A couple kids played Super Mario 3, some played on the computers, and a few watched "Jurassic Park 3." I didn't even know there was a "Jurassic Park 3."

A kid asked me what kind of music I like. I made him guess. "Punk rock?" I was a little surprised. Then he said, "So, you're one of them?"

"One of them?"

"Yeah, a punk rocker?" I said I guess so. He asked if I was vegetarian. I told him I was vegan and explained what that meant. Another kid asked me if my house stank. He said all vegetarians' houses stink.

2003 was the start of bad times for these schools.

A dismal state economy lead to devastating budget cuts. One estimate showed a loss of $2.4 million for the city and $95 million statewide. There were plans to shorten the school year. We already had one of the shortest school year in the nation. The proposed three week roll back would put schools woefully below the federal minimum for instruction hours. Those days would be have to be added to the next year, despite operating under the same budgetary constraints, or they'd lose federal funding. Teachers would be laid off and classroom sizes would grow to unmanageable numbers, art and music classes would be decimated, and sports would be dropped altogether. Talented and Gifted and special ed. would get hit extra hard. Special ed. teachers were expected to continue to teach their classes and deal with the mounds of paper work without knowing where they would be placed next year if they got to keep their job. A last ditch effort tax increase ballot measure was defeated by voters. There was no money anywhere. Things looked bleak. Then the government declared another war. I know a huge, Byzantine beauracracy keeps the money designated for war separate from the money for education, but it's still upsetting to know that the amount spent on the one Patriot Missile that was downed by friendly fire would have been enough to cover the budget cuts for the year.

Frustration was mounting. There was going to be a big rally for more funding for education at the state capital building in Salem. Having no other way to get there, I decided to hitchhike down.

Iris came with me. She used to live in the capital city and wanted an excuse to go back. We got a late start. After a couple hours of getting nothing but middle fingers and invectives, it was starting to get dark. We were about to call it quits when finally someone stopped. As Iris and I neared the car, he drove off. If you've ever hitchhiked, you're familiar with that trick. But here's a new twist on an old favorite: as the car pulled away, the car behind him smashed into it at 45 miles per hour. This was clearly karmic retribution for hitchhikers everywhere. Iris and I bolted.

In retrospect, I guess sticking around to see if everyone was ok would have been the right thing to do, but the way I figured it, some guy who was already antagonistic towards us just got rear-ended. I didn't want to hang around and hear what he had to say to us.

Iris and I had run about three blocks when it dawned on me: maybe this guy wasn't pulling the "let's make them run and then speed off" trick. Maybe he really stopped for us and only took off because he saw a car barreling towards him in his rear view mirror. We went back to check it out.

As it turns out, the guy who got hit was really nice. As soon as he saw us he asked if we were ok. When we returned the question he said, "It's just the car. I'm glad no one got hurt." Then he apologized for not being able to give us a ride. How nice is that? I felt like a big jerk for running away.

I offered my phone number to both drivers in case they needed a witness. They said the police would be here soon. I decided to slip away. A hitchhiker with a can of spray paint and some stencils probably wasn't someone the cops were going to warm up to. Besides, a girl who had stopped to make sure everything was ok offered us a ride. She was driving to the capital to visit her boyfriend, who, luck would have it, used to bully Iris in high school.

After milling around a bit, we tracked down Iris's friend and stayed at his house. My hopes of getting to sleep on the couch were dashed when we got there and saw Iris's friend's housemate was ill and had taken it over. He said I could take his bed, though, which turned out to be a dubious offer. It was the grittiest bed in which I've ever slept. I couldn't figure out why, there's no beach for over a hundred miles. Maybe he spent the day at the gravel pit and rolling around on the floor of a lumber mill. That's probably why he's sick. I don't mean to be unappreciative. It was better than walking around all night, and it was better than the time I tried to sleep on the ground at an unfinished truck stop somewhere between Reno and Salt Lake City. But still, it grossed me out. I put my jacket back on and used my sweater instead of the pillow, but I still had trouble sleeping.

After a quick breakfast, Iris and I took off for the rally. It was tamer than I expected. I knew it was all teachers and principals, I knew I wasn't going to see a Reclaim the Streets action or kids in balaclavas waving red and black flags. I did expect some yelling, though, or at least a fiery speech or two. I started to feel out of place. This feeling was compounded when I noticed lots of people had these nice, neat signs with messages like, "Think about our children" or something about spending more money on education and less on trying to get a major league baseball team.

Meanwhile, Iris and I were using a ripped piece of cardboard and a sharpie to make a sign for our trip home.

As the rally dwindled down, Iris and I headed to the on-ramp, our newly made sign in tow. It didn't take long to get picked up this time. As I got in the car I realized the driver was an education assistant at a school in which I sub frequently. She only stopped because she recognized me. I take great pains to keep my deadbeat punk side hidden from my co-workers and now I was exposed. It was awkward. What could I say? "You know, after a tough week of working with kids, sometimes I like to kick back by hitchhiking with trannies. Would you care for a bite of this candy bar I stole last night?"

My Third Year

September 2002
to
June 2003

Clouster Elementary school
September 4, 6

My first day back to work started 15 hours after my plane landed after being out of town for a month and a half. I thought I had another week before the school year started. I wasn't too happy about that. Plus I got a flat tire on my ride to work. Luckily the day was easy. I worked in the fourth and fifth grade behavior problem room in which I subbed before. The teacher, for whatever reason, thought I was cool. Last time I was here she asked me if I was a musician or if I just looked like one. I figured playing drums is almost like being a musician, so I said yes.

I got no such dubious compliments this time. I mostly made photocopies and helped kids with word searches. Friday, the 6th, was a half day, which means I did the same things I did on Wednesday, only half as much.

Freeman Middle School
September 10

The kids remembered me. That's always a satisfying feeling. Well, not always. It's satisfying when they remember liking me.

Taft High School
September 11, 12, 13

This was the life skills class I subbed in tons of times. They wanted me to take this position permanently. I had to turn it down. I really liked the kids in this class, but I had a hard time with the teacher. She was very strict and difficult to work with. The teacher tried to guilt me into staying all year. She had the kids ask me to stay, and when I still declined she asked if it was her fault.

I played basketball with the students, which really just involved me jumping in front of a kid and waving my arms wildly in front of him and then knocking the ball out of his hand. He loved it.

Henwood Middle School
September 18

This was the autism/communication behaviors class. That means the students were pretty severely autistic. A few kids were non-verbal, the rest had pretty low verbal skills. They could repeat things that were said to them (or things they saw in a movie a few weeks ago), but couldn't express how they were feeling or what they wanted. That's where the "behaviors" part of the class came in. I can't imagine how frustrating it would be to not be able to communicate something like "I need some space" or "I'm uncomfortable" or even "I'm hungry" or "I have to poop," especially if someone was waving a book in my face and telling me it's story time or trying to make me sit down. Understandably, the kids would blow out. (Not to knock the teachers; I thought they were doing really well in balancing school work and figuring out the students' needs.)

There were nine students and seven staff and it was still a rough day. It was early in the school year and a lot of details were still being worked out, programs tested. There was a lot of yelling and running around, mostly from the students. One kid was a biter, spitter, and hair-puller. I got gleeked on once, but managed to stay out of arm's (and teeth's) reach. At recess, the other EA pointed out there were nine kids, but none of them were playing with each other. They were all preoccupied separately.

Clouster Elementary school
September 19
        Legos........

Apollo Site
September 20
        This is the school for the worst behavioral problem high schoolers in the district. This is their last stop in the district. The classrooms are in this weird building in this desolate industrial area, by the river, kind of by the airport, removed from everything. The bike ride there was awful. I was pedalling down narrow streets with no shoulders and semi-trucks roaring by me. I thought I was going to die.

I got placed in a room with a substitute teacher. Two subs in a room of the toughest kids in the district, this was going to be great. Before the students arrived the other EA told us about the class and gave us the rundown on what to expect today. Students were probably going to walk into me or bump me to challenge me. I should ignore it, but I shouldn't move out of their way. They were going to get up and leave the room. I was to follow them but I wasn't to touch them or bother trying to talk them into coming back to class. However, I was told to keep them out of the teachers' lounge, where they would try to use the phone, possibly to call family or gang members to come kick somebody's ass or worse. I asked what I should do if they left the building. "They're not going to leave. They have no where to go but home, and that's even worse than here for them."

I was told to be careful in PE, they're probably going to throw basketballs at my head. Only one student was allowed in the bathroom at a time. The tanks of the toilets were tied down so the kids couldn't tamper with them and there was a sign on the door saying substitutes couldn't go in after a student alone for fear of accusations of sexual misconduct.

My classroom was the ODCD Room - Oppositional Defiant Confrontational Disorder. The EA said, "As bad as it can get, I'm glad I'm not on the other side of the building." I found out that side was for sexually abused kids.

I braced myself for a terrible day, but it wasn't so bad. I didn't really do much and the kids ignored me all day. There were no blow-ups or fights or any real problems. There was no teaching or learning going on either. The kids just teased each other and used lots of profanity.

There were six kids the first half of the day and three the second. Early on a student told me I looked scared. Really, my body was tense not because I was worried, but because I was holding back flatulence. It's a dangerous situation. One fart, even the most wee of pips, would ruin me, especially within the first hour of the day. If a kid hears that, you're finished. You might as well have walked in wearing your pants up past your belly button and tape on the middle of your glasses, or Zubaz pants and an Amy Grant "Hearts in Motion" tour shirt.

The last three hours were spent watching *Smoke Signals* and Michael Jackson videos. I couldn't believe the kids were into it. I'm still a young man, and after working with kids for a few years I thought I had a grasp on what was cool and what wasn't. Then I watched Michael Jackson spin, grab his crotch and emit a squeal unbefitting a castrati and heard a kid say in hushed, reverential tones, "That was *tight*!" and I had to rethink everything. How out of touch am I? Maybe walking in with an Amy Grant shirt would score you cred, I just don't know anymore.

DuBois Middle School
September 23 - 25

This was a behavior problem room. The teacher was strict (an ex-cop) but a nice guy. I went through reading, spelling, and language arts lessons with three students at a time. I also administered a three minute math test. A kid asked me what kid of music I like. I told him punk. For the rest of the day he called me punk. "I'm done, punk," "It's your turn, punk."

Lowery Elementary School/Zulueta Middle School
October 28

      I got called to Lowery Elementary School for the first half of the day and Zulueta Middle school for the last half. I biked 120 blocks to Lowery and got there an hour late. Though the teacher was really nice to me, she was so mean to the students it made me uncomfortable. "That was a stupid answer." "Hello! Think!" I wanted to work with the kids just so I could show them not all teachers are jerks, but I ended up just grading papers and making copies.

      After a quick, unsatisfying lunch, I biked 150 blocks to Zulueta. I got there to discover the address I had was out-dated. The building I was at used to house Zulueta Middle School until they found asbestos all over. I had to call my boss from a payphone (I had no cash, per usual, and had to use my calling card) and get the right address. Then I got lost and ended up in an industrial area. Trucks were whizzing by, nearly hitting me; then it started to rain. Two and a half hours after leaving Lowery I finally got to Zulueta. I was an hour and a half late, wet, exhausted and in a foul mood.

      This was also a behavior problem room. I sat next to a squirrely kid and kept him focussed on his work. Then I played Uno with a kid. He cheated, so I started cheating, too.

Zulueta Middle School
October 29

      Back to the same behavior room. The other EA brought cake and coffee from the teachers' lounge for the kids. I thought that was a bad idea.

Henwood Elementary School
October 30

      The other EA looked like an R. Crumb drawing.

Murray Elementary School
October 31

      I requested an elementary school today hoping I'd be there for a Halloween party. I even brought a mask. I got sent to one, but my class went on a field trip

I got to work late, but just in time to catch the secretary giving a student a ride to Star Base to meet up with the rest of his class. I locked up my bike and got in her car. It was a weird ride, the secretary drove and the student and I sat in the back seat. Luckily he warmed up to me quickly.

Star Base is a special program at an air force base. I guess the class goes there once a week. The kids are in a classroom for math and science lessons for the first half of the day. Today's lessons were on inertia, friction, waves and graphing points. Then lunch. There was a "no thank you" table for whatever food the kids didn't want from their school brown bag lunches. It was mostly a dumping ground for the soggy carrots, but I managed to get a small banana out of it.

Next the class went to a room inside the air force base for a more hands-on class taught by guys in fatigues. The kids used phones and faxes to send and receive instructions on how to graph something. I stood at the back of the room. Soon I noticed some gory safety posters on the wall, in full view of the kids. One said, "Wear a helmet. Don't wear rings," accompanied by a photograph of a guy with a head wound and a photograph of a hand with the middle finger just bone from the knuckle down. The rest of the finger, the thimble of flesh that should have surrounded the bone, was a couple inches away, and the ring was off to the side.

When we got back to school my one-on-one asked, "Does my mom know about you? Does the court know about you?"

Peirmont Elementary School
November 4-7

The first day I played tag with kids at recess, which set a dangerous precedence. Every time I subbed at this school I had to play tag or suffer a huge guilt trip. I also pushed kids on the tire swing and pretended to puke on them. They squealed with delight. They wouldn't let me stop until my throat got sore. The next day I fake pooped on the kids, but decided that was probably going too far.

After a few days I felt I was getting the hang of this class. I don't know if that's a good thing or not. I caught myself saying things like, "This will come off your recess time."

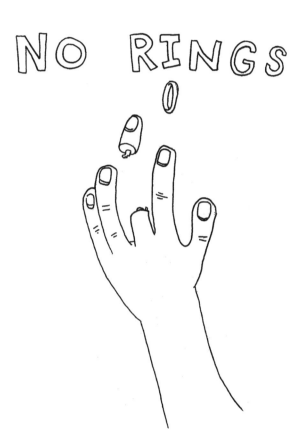

Henwood Elementary School
December 6

I got hit by a car on the way to work. It's shocking to suddenly find yourself on your back on the side of the street, the rain coming down on your face. There's that moment before pain or even embarrassment, when there's just confusion, a dumbfounded recognition of the fact that somehow your bike is now on top of you. On the positive side, both my bike and I were fine, and I was going to be late to work anyway. Now I had a good excuse. Looking back I probably could have done almost no work and the other teachers and EAs would have been sympathetic. But you know me and my strong work ethic...

Peirmont Elementary School
January 6-17

Today was the first day back after winter break. It was also the day the person I was seeing moved to another city. I wasn't in the mood to be at work, but I managed to smile through the kids showing off their Christmas gifts. A girl asked me if I had a wife. No. "You look weird. No girl will ever like you." Thanks, kid. Great timing.

I had a really good time in this class. One of my favorite jokes was to help a kid put his coat on. When he put his arm in the left sleeve I'd put my arm in the right. The kids also liked it when they'd line up for recess and instead of saying "OK, go outside," I'd look at them and say, "Get out of my face!"

One kid was insecure and took everything really personally. He'd write down the right answer for math, but he wouldn't be satisfied with the way the number looked, so he'd erase it and rewrite it. He'd do this several times for one problem. When I told him to stop, or put my hand over the problem so he couldn't erase it he'd get depressed and say, "You don't like me." He would also get upset at recess if the kids ran from him, which is something you've got to get over if you're playing tag.

I arm wrestled a kid in a wheelchair. He'd be all giggly until we started, then he'd have this serious, intent face during the match. Then he'd be all giggly again when he beat me.

One day, as I rolled up to work, I noticed all the kids outside were giggling. It wasn't a normal giggling, it was the kind that accompanies something inappropriate, like hearing the PE teacher say, "everyone give me your balls". I followed the kids' eyes and saw two huge raccoons engaged in coitus in a tree. Seeing as how there was nothing I could do, I headed inside, but not before I heard some kid say, "He's getting it on! Look at his face!" At recess I had to stop kids from throwing sticks at them. I wanted to make sure nothing interfered with their afterglow.

On my birthday I brought vegan cookies and the kids made me a birthday card. They also gave me a card and threw a party for me on my last day there. It was really sweet.

Keida Elementary School
March 31

A girl told me she lived for money. A boy asked me if I breakdance.

Keida Elementary School
April 16-18

The kids were excited to see me and the teacher was glad I was there. Then a kid made fun of my name. I took kids to a mainstream music class where they practiced their presidential rap.

Henwood Elementary School
April 21, 22, 23

I learned how to deal with a kid who has just take a big mouthful of water that he plans to spit on you: Get behind him, lead him to the sink and hold his nose.

Lowery Elementary School
May 1, 2

I worked in the k-1 room. I lifted kids to the monkey bars and held them up as the swung across. I had to stop when my glasses got knocked off the third time. On my lunch break, I saw a middle-aged couple dry-humping at the bus stop.

Kennedy High School
May 5-7

I worked in the behavior room. I played chess with a student and lost. On Tuesday I played two games of chess. I lost them both. After work I decided to stop by the chain grocery store for a few things for dinner. Money was tight and I decided to go ahead and slip something in my back-pack. I got a few other things and got in the 10 items or less the line. The woman ahead of me had 17 items. I know it's a little ridiculous for someone who is shoplifting to get upset that someone is abusing the 10 items or less policy, but it took forever for me to get through that line. Eventually I got out, but before I was ten feet from the door someone grabbed my shoulder. I got busted. Security lead my back into the store by the arm. I was mortified. I was only two blocks from the high school in which I had just subbed and there were definitely students in the store. What if one of them saw me? I was supposed to come back the next day.

I got into the back room without being seen. Now I had new worries. I knew they weren't going to arrest me, but I was still screwed. I played up my nervousness for pity, I didn't look them in the eyes and was very polite. They took a polaroid of me and my burden: a package of tofu and a candy bar. I wanted to wink at the camera, but I thought they'd get upset. They let me go, charged me for the food (which I didn't get to keep) and gave me a $250 fine. I tried to whine my way down to $100, but they weren't having it. All in all, I guess I got off easy, but the next day at work I was worried I'd hear, "Hey, didn't I see you yesterday..."

But I didn't hear anything about it the next day so I guess I'm safe. Plus, I finally beat that kid at chess.

Van Buren High School
May 8

I started out my day biking to Cope-Grey Middle School where I was to work one-on-one with a girl in a wheelchair. That involved helping her in the bathroom. The teacher and I came to the conclusion that it was probably illegal for me, a male, to help a girl in the bathroom. Even if it wasn't illegal, nobody was comfortable with it. So I got sent to Van Buren High School, which was on the other side of town. It was already 11:00 when I got there. I was to work one-on-one with a boy in a wheelchair, but no one in the office could figure out where he was. When they finally found him, he was taking off for work. That meant there was really nothing for me to do. The secretary asked if I wanted to be assigned to another school. I figured it would probably be 1:00 by the time I got to any other school. I said I'd stick around there and see if they needed help in the library. Then I checked my e-mail for a couple hours and took off early.

Ferber Elementary School
May 12- 16

This was the Life Skills with Nursing class, the lowest functioning kids in the district. There was a sub for another EA. She was nuts. We turned on music for the kids and she started dancing. I mean, like, serious dancing. She also had trouble not doing anything (unlike me, who feels no compunction in sitting idly for large parts of my work day), but she really didn't do anything useful. Also, she really didn't do what was asked of her.

It was a nurse's birthday and the Speech Pathologist had set up some games for her to compete with the kids. My favorite was the spelling bee. There were these devices that the teachers could use to record their voice and when the kids pushed a five inch button it played back. As the kids were non-verbal, these were usually used for messages like, "come play with me" or "will you read to me?" Now, however, the Speech Pathologist used them to spell out the words he gave them, like "cat" or "cake." He gave the nurse words like "hieroglyphics," "picturesque," and "unconscious."

The second day wasn't as fun. I mostly washed dishes and cleaned toys and mats. I held a girl on my lap. She got scared and her whole body stiffened up. The nurse said it wasn't my fault, but I still felt bad about it.

I tried to do some sensory stuff with the kids. Some liked having their face fanned and others liked me slapping the trays on their wheelchairs, making as loud a sound as possible. One kid in particular loved it. He would jump in his chair and then burst out laughing.

Thursday started with me changing a 17-year-old kid's shitty diaper. At the end of the day, while changing kids before they went home (or back to the hospital, really) the EAs started talking about a recent police shooting of an unarmed African-American motorist. One EA said she shouldn't have been in the wrong place at the wrong time, that she was a drug user and it didn't matter much. She then railed against the "asshole protestors" (she was using profanity freely in front of the students) who didn't have jobs but just went from protest to protest breaking things that honest, hard-working tax-payers had to pay for. I stayed quiet the rest of the day.

Zulueta Middle School
May 21

I got to work early. I was told there was going to be a sub for the teacher, but he or she hadn't showed up yet. It got close to the start of school and still no sub. I thought I might have to sub for both EA and teacher. I was nervous, but I started psyching myself up for it. I had just gotten to the point where I was not only ready but excited about taking on the whole class when the sub showed up. I felt let down.

Looking back, it was probably for the best I wasn't the only teacher in the room; the kids probably would have walked all over me. But I'm pretty sure I would have been better than the sub they got. She was crazy. She had buttoned her shirt wrong. Yeah, it's a mistake anyone can make, but when you sub, especially at a middle school, you have to give the kids as little to make fun of you about as possible. You have to double, maybe triple check your fly, bring some mints, and make sure your shirt is buttoned correctly.

She also picked out her favorite students early, and seemingly arbitrarily. And she called them the best students in front of the rest of the class. One of her favorites kept causing problems with other kids, calling them names and trying to bait them in to fights. He had autism and couldn't really help it, but he certainly didn't deserve the preferential treatment she bestowed on him. When he got really worked up, I'd take him for a walk around the school to calm him down.

When I got back the teacher was yelling at kids. Again, it seemed pretty arbitrary who she was singling out. I tried to intervene. Sure those kids were acting up, but at this point everyone was acting up, and the teacher yelling at them and threatening them didn't help. One of the kids called her racist. At first I dismissed it because I thought she was just crazy, but when I thought about it, I noticed she was favoring the white students. I felt really bad that not only did the kids have to deal with it, but at 13-years-old they were so used to it they could identify it that easily and not become totally irate. I also felt bad that I didn't notice it. I redoubled my efforts to be fair and stand up for students. I don't know if I was much use, though.

I played Sorry with the kids. For lunch I got a bag of potato chips and cheap vegan cookies and ate them while on recess duty. A kid came up and asked for a cookie. I warned him they were kind of gross but gave him one. I think that cemented my position as the cool sub. A girl said I should be the teacher, not the other sub. I felt a little better. Maybe my being there changed something.

Fairfax Elementary School
May 23

I worked in the Autism room. It wasn't as tough as the other autism class in which I worked before. These kids could speak, and though there were still some behavioral problems due to their autism, it wasn't nearly as severe as the other class. These kids were so sweet and trusting. They came up and grabbed my hand right away. I helped with an art project: the kids shaved crayons onto wax paper, then I put another sheet of wax paper over it and ironed it, melting the crayon shavings. The kids cut out the wax paper to look like butterflies.

Harrison High School
May 27

I worked in the behavior room. There was a rabbit in the class. I mean, scampering around the class, not in a cage. I talked about *Gummo* with a student. (The Harmony Korine movie, not the fifth Marx Brother who didn't make the transition from Vaudeville to movies.) I also participated in an activity in which I was blindfolded and a kid lead me to a park across the street from the school. It was some sort of social skill exercise on trusting each other. I don't know why I was included, as I didn't know these students long enough to trust them, or for them to trust me.

Taft High School
May 28-30, June 2

I was sent to the Life Skills class I worked in a million times before. The kids were excited to see me. So was the teacher. During Speech the teacher asked me to get in front of the class and tell them what I've been up to, then they'd ask me questions. It was an exercise to make sure the kids were paying attention and to help them learn how to keep a conversation going. A lot of these kids had trouble in this area, tending to just talk about specific things that interested them and not being able to handle it when the conversation went somewhere else. I told the class that I had gone on tour. Someone asked what kind of music my band played. I was glad I didn't have to go into any sub-genre and just said, "Punk rock." The teacher asked if people still "bam danced".

DuBois Middle School
June 3

I worked in the behavior room. I don't feel I did very much. I mean I didn't do much academic stuff. I finished four crossword puzzles and wrote in my journal. A kid asked me what I was writing. I told him I keep a journal and that every once in a while I rewrite some stuff and put it out and that I got to go on tour with it. He seemed pretty interested. He asked if he could read what I was writing. I said he probably couldn't read my handwriting. The first word he saw that he could decipher was "sex". I told him it said "set", but I don't think he believed me.

Taft High School
June 5-6, 9-10

This was the same class I was in a week ago. We were going on a field trip to Mersey Park for a picnic. Before we left, I took a couple kids with me to a nearby grocery store and picked up some vegan food. I sat by the pond with a student while we ate. He would point to the ducks and say, "Look! That's you!" I'd wait until the ducks put their heads under water and point to their asses and say, "There's you!" He'd point to a dog, I'd point to a squirrel. It went on for a while.

I took the kids to get recycling on Monday. They went around the school and picked up all the bags full of cans. Every so often, they take the bags to get recycled and use the money for something for the classroom.

On the last day of school, the class took a little field trip. It was something the teacher had decided that morning, and she hadn't really prepared for it. It was a frustrating morning. First she had me take the kids outside while she got ready, then changed her mind and had the other EA come out to tell me she was going on the field trip and I was staying behind to take a student to his mainstream art class. When I got back to the room the lights were out and the door was locked. The student was already in his class and the teacher had taken off. I didn't know which art class my student was in and, seeing as I didn't have keys, I couldn't get into the room to check his schedule. I didn't know what to do. I even tried using a credit card to break into the room but it didn't work. Even the most rudimentary of planning could have prevented this. Eventually, and only with the help of another teacher, I got into the classroom and tracked my student down. His class was watching *O, Brother, Where Art Thou?*, not really something he needed my help with.

My Fourth Year

September 2003
to
April 2004

Taft High School
September 3 - 24

This was the class in which I was offered a permanent job at the beginning of last school year. I turned it down because I didn't think I could get along with the teacher. The person they ended up hiring quit so I guess I made the right call. Again they offered me the job permanently. Again I declined. But I did work her for the first few weeks

September 3

The halls were almost empty on the first day of school as it was a freshmen only day. It was heartbreaking to see all these freshman, awkward in their adolescence, acting like they owned these halls, anxiety thinly veiled as bravado. Tomorrow, when the upperclassmen come, things were going to be very different. I got mistaken for a student twice, once by a student and once by a teacher who asked, "Are you finding your classes alright?"

September 5

I took four kids to mainstream PE. The class did hokey "let's get to know each other" games, like everybody lining up in alphabetical order or by order of their birthday. One of my students was nonverbal and two others, though verbal, couldn't understand the directions, so I had to help them through every step, each separately. The fourth student couldn't care less about the whole thing and ran to the corner. It was rough. We consistently held up the rest of the class until I decided to just put my students anywhere in the line.

Septemeber 8

After school let out, I stopped by the art room to talk to my friend who was just hired as the art teacher. We talked about how we want to let kids know we're involved in punk/DIY or whatever, but don't want to cross the adult/peer line, at least not too soon. At times I definitely feel like a hypocrite, claiming all these anti-authoritarian, non-hierarchical beliefs and threatening kids with time-outs. Even worse, there have been times I didn't even realize I was in a petty power struggle until I was in the middle of it. But I've also had times when I could put the students on my level and it's been amazing. There was the time a student was clearly having a bad day and I took him into the hall and told him I was having a bad day, too, and if he would try to help me I'd try to help him. For the rest of the day he was really nice to me. And I kept my end of the bargain and found other ways to work with him. I wish every interaction could be based on that kind of mutual trust and respect, but I have to face the fact that I *am* in a position of authority and students see me as such. I think I need to establish the adult/peer line to ensure I can put myself on the same level as the students and not have it turn into a huge mess. Then one of her students came in to get his notebook. He looked at me and said, "I think I saw a show at your house over the summer." Adult line erased.

September 11

All week I had been noticing these two girls that dress the same. They're not twins, just really good friends. The first day they wore matching camel skirts , fancy shawls, and big black boots. They were walking side by side and I think they were on cell phones, although I might be making that part up. The next day they wore blue velour running suits and after that was some sort of white outfit. I was totally fascinated by them. I tried to figure out which characters they'd be if this were a teen movie. I was torn between the weird girls who are friends with the main character, who maybe finish each other's sentences, or the ice queens who the attractive but shy (and maybe nerdy, if he's wearing glasses) boy has a crush on until he discovers the inner beauty of the shy, quirky girl.

September 16

I took a couple students on a "field trip" to a grocery store to get coffee and distilled water for the teacher. When we got back the teacher yelled at us for getting drinking water instead of distilled water. She said she couldn't drink drinking water, it tasted disgusting to her. That put me in a bad mood. She went so far as to say that getting her drinking water was tantamount to someone giving me meat. Fuck you.

After lunch, the whole class went on another "field trip" to the grocery store to exchange the drinking water for distilled water.

September 17

The class went on a field trip to the Rhododendron Gardens. We ate lunch by a pond. The ducks were quacking loudly. I told a kid they were saying, "Quack quack give me your bread quack," or, "Quack quack I'm hungry quack." At the time it was funny, honest. I said it in a duck voice. The student liked it. He asked me to say "Taft High School" like a duck. I said it, then he did. He asked me to say other things, like "steep hill" and "your car needs a carburetor adjustment." I'd say them then he would, as ducks, of course. Then he asked me to say "traffic light." "OK. Quack quack traffic light quack. Now you say it."

"Quack quack bend over for your check-up." He didn't understand why I was laughing so hard.

September 23

I took a few kids to help out at an organization that puts together meals for the needy and shut-ins. First, I supervised the packaging of meals on wheels. Then served meals to people who came in and then cleaned up afterward. Since I didn't get a lunch break I got to leave half an hour early. I was in a pretty good mood and I was glad to avoid having to push through halls crowded with students on my way out. I got to my bike and found someone had put glue in my lock. I went to the office and tried to stay as low-profile as possible while asking the secretary for something that might dissolve the glue. She got on the walkie-talkie to the janitor and said loudly, "We have a sub here and someone put glue in his bike lock!" The kids in the office looked at me. There go all my cool sub points.

I poured the solvent in and let it sit for a bit, then tried to scrape the glue out with a safety pin. It didn't work but I did manage to flick toxic solvent in my face. After an hour and a half I went back to the office. They called a teacher who lived nearby and he showed up quickly with his power saw and his 2 ½-year-old son. I felt bad for making him come back to work. I felt even worse when, immediately after cutting though my lock, his son touched the saw blade (which at this point was very hot) and burst into tears.

Faulkner Elementary School
September 25

I got called in for a half day, the last half of the day. Nice. I went back to bed. A few minutes later I was called and told to go in for the whole day. Damn.

I worked one-on-one with a kid in a wheelchair. Before the student arrived, the teacher made a big deal about me not knowing how to feed or toilet him. Another staff member stared at me dumbly when I told her I was subbing there, as if she couldn't believe they'd send someone like me.

Usually I come in figuring that although I might not be the best person for the job, I'm sure I could make it through the day alright. Everyone's reaction, however, dissolved my confidence.

The day went really well, I think. The kid's mom came to school with him and showed me how to change his diaper. (He was too big to lift on to a table so he had to be changed standing up.) I got him into his stander. We joked around a lot. The second time I changed him I had trouble peeling the tape tab on his diaper. He was braced on my left shoulder and the tape was on his right side, where I couldn't see it. And I had latex gloves on, so I couldn't feel what I was doing. While I was struggling to hold him up and open the tape, his former assistant came by. He knocked on the bathroom door. "Come on! Hurry up in there!... You need help?... Hurry up!... What's taking so long?..." Thanks, friend. As if maybe I was just savoring the experience of squatting on a bathroom floor holding up a kid whose rapidly losing strength and starting to fall on me while I'm putting on his diaper, thanks for yelling at me every three seconds.

Keida Elementary School
September 26, 30

One girl was really clingy. She kept grabbing and hugging me. It was sweet at first, but quickly turned annoying. I'd try to chase down a kid who had run away from the story circle and as I'd pass her she'd grab my legs. One of her big things was untying her shoes so someone would have to tie them, giving her more attention. The fifth or sixth time she did it I told her this was the last time I was going to do this. I sat her down and started to tie her shoes and she sneezed in my face. I decided to take my 15 minute break right then.

Baldwin Elementary School
October 2

This is a school for worst behavior problem elementary school students in the district. I got a sense that at 9- and 10-years-old these kids were already nearing the end of their childhood. The infallibility of their parents and the normalcy of their lives hadn't been questioned yet. They still had hope and innocence. But these qualities were fading away, getting replaced with the confusion, anger, and desperation of one given a reponsibility he doesn't understand and for which he isn't equipped.

I waited for something to go wrong, but nothing did. There were

o minor incidents, but nothing major. A kid asked a teacher if she was a les-
an. She overreacted. "I'm offended by that, and I'm sure my son and daugh-
r would be offended by that." Way to show the kids that being called gay is
horrible insult, you fucking dolt.

The other incident was a kid crawling under the teacher's desk, pushing
e drawers out and sitting up in their place. That way he couldn't be pulled
t. He also claimed he couldn't get out because it was too splintery. Two men
m the coaches' room (which is what they call the detention room when the
ole school is the detention room) came by, but, short of lifting the desk over
m, there was nothing they could do. The kid's mother was called in. She
abbed his ankles, pulled him out and left.

One of my jobs was walking students to the bathroom. One student was
ally polite. He even thanked me for walking with him. I can only imagine
at he's like when things go too far and he snaps. While the kids were in the
throom I had time to admire the mural in the hallway. It was a cityscape, with
s of giant apes and the occasional wolf thrown in for good measure.

Early on I was asked to sit with a kid as he did math. He just needed
ot of redirection. Without it he'd get distracted and the next thing you know
would be doing the splits next to his desk. He was a sweet kid, though. I
lped him work on his writing assignment. He'd write a line and I'd write two
es. Next was reading. He'd read a page and a half and I'd read a half.

I was only called in for a half day, so I got ready to leave at 12:30. The
I had been working with asked me why I had to leave. What could I say?
ey're not paying me for a full day so I'm not working a full day? I gave a non-
swer and grabbed my coat. Before I left he asked, "Bear hug?" It broke my
art.

ida Elementary School
tober 3, 6-8, 13-16

Back to the K-1 class. The kids were extra whiny today and they kept
tting each other off. Quiet time was the worst. All the kids would stand up,
l or moan. Another kid imitated everything the other kids did, so if one kid
ed, he'd fake cry. If a kid yelled, he yelled. It was really frustrating. Then a
l drooled on her chair on purpose.

When I came in on Monday the secretary called me "reliable Dave." At
st I thought she was being facetious because I was late again, but then I fig-
d it must be because I sub here so often. Later I found out I was right the
st time.

During choosing one kid pretended he was a robot. Apparently he was an evil robot, because he destroyed other kids' Lego houses and stomped on Matchbox cars.

Despite having a long night of kind of calling it quits with someone I was seeing, I actually made it to work on time on Tuesday. I was tired and depressed, though, and didn't have a lot of patience. An hour or so into the day I decided I had to snap out of it. These kids got enough negative attention and I was determined to be the fun sub. I bounced kids on my knee and chased them around at recess. I also didn't get them in trouble when they acted up. We all have shit going on, right?

As I walked back to school from my lunch break I saw the other class in which I sub frequently at recess. Six kids stopped their game and ran over to say hi to me. It put me in a good mood.

The bike ride to work on Wednesday was beautiful. It was overcast, but there was just enough of a clearing to the east to let the sunrise in. The tops of the trees took on honeyed tones, starkly contrasting the grey nimbus backdrop. The ionized air was rich with the smell of impending rain. I took the side streets and rode slow just to savor it. Then it started raining, not hard, just enough to speed me up.

I got to work early, before the teacher. I wasn't given keys so I hung around outside the classroom awkwardly with a student and his dad.

Over the weekend I was kind of sick. My sinuses were all stuffed up. I had this great idea that if I ate something hot, say, a habañero, it would clear me out. Though it felt as though I were eating molten glass, my sinuses were unaffected. My left nostril and eye were affected, however, when I rubbed them before washing my hands. It was a rough night.

On Monday morning I figured my habañero woes were behind me. Then I went to the bathroom. It was a bad scene. The bike ride to work was extra painful. Somehow I made it to work on time, but I was fully prepared to explain myself if I hadn't. "I'm sorry I'm late today. I ate habañeros last night and when I pooped this morning it felt as though someone had kicked a beehive into my asshole."

It was a student's birthday on Sunday, so we had a little party for him at the end of the day on Monday. Another student got really upset and cried because it wasn't his birthday.

Later in the week some kids were teasing a girl about having a boyfriend. The girl, who was maybe 6-years-old, got up and said, super sassily, "I don't need a boyfriend!"

Fairfax Elementary School
October 17

I worked in the autism room. The kids didn't really play with each other at recess, but they were into me chasing them around. When I stopped to catch my breath I noticed one of the students standing by the slide, pants around his ankles, peeing into the wood chips.

Kennedy High School
October 20

During reading I stood around and watched the kids get into small groups. After ten minutes I realized I was supposed to be teaching one of these groups.

O'Connor Middle School
October 21

Most of the day I just helped a boy in a wheelchair get prepared at the beginning of his classes, pack up at the end, and sit around and write in my journal in between. In his third period class, a boy with a homemade Exploited patch (the sharpie and an old T-shirt kind) on his denim jacket and a punk girl kept looking at me, probably because I'm so unhideably and undeniably punk. During lunch my student asked me if I liked South Park. I veered the conversation over to "The Simpsons". He asked if I liked anime. I said I had seen *Princess Mononoke*. He asked what kind of music I liked. I told him punk. He was excited by that. "Linkin Park? Korn? Good Charlotte?"

I took my student to PE. I was really worried he might get hurt, but my fear was assuaged when I learned the class was playing golf. Not even middle school boys can turn golf into a contact sport. I took him to his bus a few minutes early. We talked more about South Park. He said, "Maybe you'll come back tomorrow. That would be cool." That totally made up for the fact that the teacher I checked in with at the beginning of the day and the secretary were amazingly rude to me.

Friday October 24

I didn't feel like going to work today, so I didn't. That's one of the benefits of being a sub. I don't even have to make up an excuse or pretend I'm sick.

Freeman Middle School
October 27

I took the class to PE. One kid kept putting his hands in my pockets. Then he got in trouble for touching a girl's butt. I took him out to the hall to try to calm him down. He banged on the lockers and tried to run into other rooms. I took him for a walk around the playground. That worked a little better.

Cope-Grey Middle School
October 29

The day went OK, I guess. Kids either liked me or didn't listen to me. I mean the same kid would go back and forth.

Tyler High School
October 30

My class went on a bowling field trip. Life skills classes from all over the city came to bowl. I saw kids I had worked with all over the place. Everyone seemed to be having a really good time. As my student had next to no use of one arm and limited use of the other, I set up a ramp for him to roll his bowling ball down. I wasn't very good at lining it up right, but I managed to avoid gutter balls.

Van Buren High School
October 31

I worked with a student who, for complicated reasons, didn't have a classroom. I met him at his cab and led him to the cafeteria and started with math: naming coins and their values, counting blocks. Then we went to band. We both sat back and listened to the band play "The Monster Mash", "The Addams Family", and "Louie, Louie". Then there was a pep assembly. As it was Halloween, a lot of kids wore costumes. The girls tended to wear skimpy costumes. I wanted to yell, "It's 40 degrees, go put some pants on."

November 3

I read in the paper that a student from a class I used to sub in frequently was shot and killed in a nearby park. I don't want to get into that maudlin "a talented young man taken from us before his prime" stuff. The kid tended to sleep through the two periods in my class so I never got to know him. But still, news like that rips through you.

Knox High School
November 5-7

The day started badly. I had a tough bike ride to school, then realized I had left my keys at home when I tried to lock it up. I had to bring it in and keep it in the office. The secretary didn't seem like she wanted to be bothered with me. The principal gave me very vague directions to the weight room, where the student with whom I was to work one-on-one was, and I got lost. I asked another teacher. She directed me to a locked door. Luckily a student showed me where to go, but it turns out my student wasn't even there. I ran into another EA who finally showed me where my student was. I was working with the student I'd had some trouble with two years ago. And I had to take him to the bathroom immediately. It wasn't even 10:00 and I was ready to call it a day.

In the bathroom he had a little smear in his underwear. He asked me to help him clean it. I'm a saint. Actually, I helped party because I could sympathize. I was afraid I had shit my pants on the bike ride to work. (It turned out I hadn't.)

Despite the frustrating morning, things went OK. The student had matured a lot since I worked with him last. He wasn't constantly being creepy to girls.

I found a quicker, less hilly route to work the next day and it took me less than an hour. I got there right as my student's bus pulled up. First period my student did clock worksheets and I did the New York Times crossword puzzle. Then we took a field trip to the Convention Center. We got to go underground and check out all the drab concrete hallways where people do the actual work of putting on conventions. Then over to the mall for lunch. I helped my student get a sandwich, then sat with him and ate my pasta with nutritional yeast.

We got back to school in time for biology. I helped him take notes. The last 15 minutes was silent reading, so I read *The Optimist's Daughter*.

I took my student to PE the next day. He shot baskets in a lower hoop. He couldn't use one of his arms, so he had this method of rolling the ball up his face with one hand and shooting. He made most of his shots. It was amazing.

I read the newspaper in the school library during my lunch break, then took my student and his girlfriend (and I use that term very loosely) to a nearby taco place for their lunch. I got french fries, the only vegan item on the menu. My student paid for everything, but later, when his girl-friend wasn't around, I gave him money for my food.

I had to take him to the bathroom. I waited outside while he pooped, then I had to wipe. He was laughing the whole time. He thought it was hysterical, which I guess is better than being embarrassed. "How do you like that, Dave?... Are you having fun?" I told him it definitely wasn't the highlight of my week.

We got to Biology late. My student didn't have his homework. The teacher told him to type up the notes. He didn't have his laptop. The teacher didn't seemed too thrilled to have this student in his class. I took him to find the laptop. He told me the person I was subbing for had a hall locker in which he kept the laptop. He just couldn't remember the combi-nation or which locker. He narrowed it down to four lockers. I went to the office, but without knowing the exact locker they couldn't help us. We went back to class laptopless and did nothing.

Hurley Elementary School
November 12

This was a Life Skills with Nursing class. It went as it usually does: slow. I helped lift kids from their chairs to the diaper changing table, wiped down mats and toys with a disinfectant. The class did an art project. Or more accurately, the staff did art projects, sometimes holding the students' hands in theirs as they cut, glued, and folded. We made turkey masks out of big paper bags and construction paper. I gave my turkey big black eye-brows and brown glasses. I hadn't gone into this project intending to make my turkey look like me, but I thought it was funny.

After my lunch break (in which I read *The Palm-Wine Drinkard* in the teachers' lounge), I sat with a kid at a computer. There was a special switch that was a little knobby thing on a spring that acted like a mouse click when she'd hit it. The next kid had a big button, maybe 6-inches in diameter, that was set up so he could push his head into it. There was a story or song and when they'd click, the page would turn or the next verse would be sung.

Student Services Building
November 13

This was a building that was mostly used for administrative pur-poses but housed a few classes for behavior problem students. I got to class kind of early, gearing myself up for a tough day. Then I saw the name tags on the desks and realized I knew some of the students, and that this wasn't a behavior class but a transition class for 18- to 21-year-old kids.

I ended up recognizing most of the class from subbing in their high school classes last year. I took a kid on the bus to the transition class at the state university. At first he didn't want me to go with him, but when he finally accepted that I was going to be the one to take him, he warmed up and talked to me the whole way to the bus stop.

When I got back to the Student Services Building class, the kids were getting taught about food safety so they could get their food handler's card. For math I sat with a girl as she picked out items from a grocery store circular, added up the prices, and gave me the amount in fake money.

Keida Elementary School
November 14

The kids were excited to see me. I got several hugs. I chased kids around during recess. One kid put his head down and walked into me. He wasn't trying to be violent, that's just what he does. I grabbed him to stop him from headbutting me. He started swinging his arms, punching. I grabbed his arms to try to protect myself. Another teacher on recess duty accused me of playing rough with him, as if I was encouraging him to punch at my gonads.

When I got back from my lunch the kids were watching "Reading Rainbow". There was a segment about making bowling balls. The whole class cheered raucously for the montage of strikes at the end of the piece.

O'Connor Middle School
November 18

I'll never work here again. All day long I had the feeling the staff thought I was an idiot. The teacher I worked with never gave me any sort of instructions, so I didn't do much. I was leading reading groups but had no idea where anything was or what I was supposed to do. The students had to tell me how to do it. I watched kids do worksheets, then I watched kids type. What am I doing here?

A kid told me his uncle (or maybe it was his grandfather, he didn't know) was going to pick him up after school, but he didn't have a note from his mom. I had to take the kid to the counselor to see if this was ok. She didn't want to help me. She said the teacher should be doing this, and sent me to the secretary.

The secretary reluctantly helped me. The name the student gave wasn't on his safe list. I went back to class and told the teacher the kid couldn't go with his uncle/grandfather. He sent me with the student back to the office. The secretary totally ignored us while she finished her conversation. Then she was really condescending to my student. She misinterpreted what was being asked, brushed me off when I tried to clarify, then gave false information. I went back to class and reported what I could to the teacher. I think he was upset with me. He told me to take over the class while he called the office. Again, he didn't explain what I was taking over so the students had to tell me what was going on. It was really frustrating. My job would be so much better if I didn't have to deal with all these adults.

Kennedy High School
November 19

I spent first period in the math resource room. The teacher introduced me to the class and had me tell them what I like to do in my spare time. I really appreciated that. It gave the students a chance to see that I'm a person and not just some weird guy standing at the back of the room. I said I play drums in a band. Two kids excitedly shot back, "I play guitar!" A girl asked me what kind of music my band played. I said punk. Then I noticed she had a Rancid sticker on her trapper keeper. She asked if we had a cd. "No, but we might make a demo tape soon." She asked if we were going to get rich and famous. "Uh, no, I don't think that's going to happen." Maybe I should have said that's not why I play music, to me punk is about blah blah blah, but I bored myself just thinking about it.

I floated around the room helping kids with their math assignments. That girl asked for help. I pointed to the Rancid sticker and said, "I saw those guys," which is usually something I say in confessional tones. She said she wanted to see Good Charlotte last night. Um, so first you have to subtract seven from both sides of the equation...

I spent the rest of the day in the A-room. Things were easy until last period. One kid threw paper at another, things escalated. I'd seen stuff like this before. Words are exchanged, then kids, without expressing it verbally, realize they're making a big deal out of nothing and it blows over. This time a fist fight broke out.

Kennedy High School
November 20, 21

I worked in the behavior room. I helped a kid with his science worksheets. I thought I was doing too much for him by telling him where he could find the answers (specifically what page and column) but then the teacher came over and gave him the answers. Later I helped him with his paper on water pollution. He said he was going to just download an essay from the internet. I told him he'd have to pay for that. In the end he copied down the free descriptions of the essays and rewrote them. He thought he was cheating, but really he was doing research. I didn't want to burst his bubble, though.

The last period was study hall. Two kids watched music videos on the computer. I walked by. "Is that Insane Clown Posse?" "You know who they are?!?" They were so excited I knew who they were I decided not to tell them I found it unfathomable a band could be worse than ICP.

The next day two kids nearly got in a fight. I made sure to get in the middle and separate them this time.

During study hall one kid watched a video and the rest played on the computers. A kid called another kid's favorite band "gay." I asked him not to use that word as an insult.

"Does it offend you?"

"Yes."

"Why does it offend you?"

I got the feeling the kid wanted me to say, "Because I'm gay." I told him why I found it offensive. (I'll assume everyone reading this knows why it's not ok to use gay as an insult. If you don't, send me an e-mail and we'll discuss it.) He said, "Well, you have the right to be offended by it and I have the right not to care."

I said that's true, but I wasn't telling him he couldn't say something but asking him as a favor not to say something I find offensive. He said, "Maybe," or "I'll think about it" or something like that, which I assume meant, "OK, but I'm not going to admit I'm wrong in front of my friends." That was fine with me. You have to take any victory, no matter how small.

The teacher asked me to rent a movie during my lunch break and she'd reimburse me. Let me get this straight, you want me to rent a movie and hand it over to a stranger who will give it to the B-room (where the students themselves admitted there was a stealing problem) and you'll pay me back even though I don't know when or if I'll ever be back. Yeah... no.

Fairfax Elementary School
December 2

This was the autism room. A kid read to me from *Healing the Dragon*. He functioned above his age academically. He made the claim, "I'm 10-years-old but I have the brain of an 11½-year-old."

Van Buren School
December 5

I worked with the kid without a classroom. I had a tote-bag with all my students worksheets and materials and worked with him in the cafeteria. Math was counting and number recognition and coins. Then we went through community sign flash cards. I had my student type on a computer in the library for a while, then we went into an empty classroom and he drew and watched "Aladdin."

Tyler High School
December 6

The class went on a field trip to the Festival of Trees, which is a big event where companies and stores sponsor Christmas trees and decorate them. For example, an auto parts store might decorate a tree with car ornaments. The Lego version of the city was cool; the clown was not. After looking at a handful of trees, a student and I sat and ate for the remaining three hours.

Kennedy High School
December 8

An EA referred to a short African-American student as "a little colored girl." What? Is this 1948?

Taft High School
December 10

I biked to work in the rain. I put my rain gear and backpack in the storage room behind the classroom. The teacher went back to get something. In front of the class she said, "Something smells back here... I think it's your stuff, Dave." I let it pass. A few minutes later she said it again. "Maybe something got mildew-y. It really smells."

"I don't think so. I keep the stuff in my house and my house doesn't smell." She reluctantly let it drop.

She had me go get a head rest for a wheelchair from a room on the other side of the school. When I came back she asked, "Where's the strap?" I wasn't told to get a strap and I don't know how these things work. She sent the other EA to get it, which made me feel dumb and useless. It wasn't even second period yet and I was really annoyed.

Then she brought up the smell for the third time. "It's coming from over here," she said while waving her arms above my stuff. Then she picked up my rain pants and sniffed them. She smelled my rain pants. Then she smelled my gloves. That's when I decided I was never coming back to this class again. It didn't help matters when she asked the kid in the wheelchair (who was nonverbal and had no gross motor control), "Did you brush your teeth this morning?" again, in front of the class. This kid couldn't possibly brush his own teeth, so it's not his fault if they weren't brushed. I wanted to advocate for the kid, but at this point I was so upset I knew I couldn't be civil so I stayed quiet.

Van Buren High School
December 11, 12

I worked one-on-one with the kid without a classroom again. First period was band. I read *Look for My Obitua*ry while listening to the kids play. Then flashcards and coin recognition.

My student was really friendly and tried to make conversation, but he would ask the same questions over and over again ("What did you have for dinner last night?" "How many brothers do you have?") or ask questions he knew the answer to ("Is it second period?" "Are we doing math?"). We took a walk after lunch. He pointed to a pile of mud and asked, "What's that?"

"Oh! I can't believe you pooped here!" He was shocked, but he loved it. He kept asking, so I kept going. "Couldn't you have waited until we got back to school? That's disgusting!"

While walking back to school my student said he was going to get me. He ran up and touched my back. I'm used to kids saying they're going to get me and, even though they're joking around, I still get my glasses swatted off or punched in the gut. This was the gentlest version of "getting" me yet. Later, he threatened to get me again. "No way, you can't get me." Then I noticed he had drool on his hand as he ran at me. I looked on my back where he had touched me earlier; there was a smear of saliva.

Kennedy High School
December 15

Back to the behavior room. There was a sub for the teacher. The teacher didn't leave any lesson plans, so there wasn't much for us to do. I guess the kids wouldn't have done the assignments anyway, but at least there would have been some structure to the class. The sub brought in *Scratch*, a documentary about scratching and hip-hop. Surprisingly the kids weren't into it. Even more surprising: some of the kids were into the movie *Around the World in 80 Days*.

Torres Elementary School
December 16

I helped kids make Santa Claus faces with beads. Later in the day one kid told the others I was his dad. He was African-American, so it wasn't a very convincing lie, but I played along.

Kennedy High School
December 18, 19

Some teachers are calling tests "celebrations of your knowledge." That's even stupider than referring to cats as "fur friends."

Fairfax Elementary School
January 5

The bike ride to school was absolutely miserable. It was freezing with a strong headwind whipping powdery snow into my face. I got to school really late. I played with plastic whales, sharks, and a sea lion during choosing, but I didn't do much more than that. I don't think the teacher trusted me very much. She had me do things that didn't involve students, like photocopying. I felt kind of useless. I guess all those worksheets will be used some time, but I still felt like I wasn't needed or particularly wanted there.

I wasn't looking forward to coming back the next day. I lied in bed as long as I could. It was so nice and warm there and so cold in my basement bedroom. I finally pulled the covers off my face. A roseate glow poured in through the windows, the kind that only accompanies some sort of precipitation. It had snowed. I felt like a kid again. I jumped out of bed, raced upstairs, and flipped the TV on. I watched the scroll at the bottom intently until finally: "Public schools-- all closed". Yes! I celebrated by having chocolate chips for breakfast. The freezing rain covered everything in ice that shut down most of the city for several days. There was no school for the rest of the week. My childlike glee at having another week off turned to old man worry about being able to pay rent and buy food with another week of not getting paid.

Henwood Elementary School
January 12

I got called for work at 7:55, ten minutes after school started. I couldn't bike too fast because the main streets were covered in aggregate and the side streets were still slushy and icy. I got to work really late, of course. A girl came up to me and asked, "Are you OK?" I thought she was referring to the scar on my left arm, but then she kissed my right arm. I guess it's just an autism thing, something she picked up somewhere and was repeating. She kissed my hand several times throughout the day. Once she tried to kiss my face, but I ducked away just in time.

I sat with kids at the sensory table, which was full of paper shreddings. It was a good tactile experience for kids. It was also good ammunition.

Then the kids went to a separate room where they could ride on trikes or jump on a little trampoline. It was kind of like indoor recess but with the purpose of improving kids' gross motor skills.

Cope-Grey Middle School
January 13 -16

I got called to the Behavior room. I was told the position was going to be open for a long time. I asked if I could try it out for a few days before I committed to the whole time.

Things went well. The first day I graded some spelling tests and took a few kids down to their health class. It was sex education time. I can't believe how smoothly that went. Then I had recess duty. The slush kept the kids inside, so I did a crossword puzzle in the gym and tried not to get hit by any basketballs. The last period of the day was Earned Activity Time, which is free time except it's predicated on good behavior. Kids played wrestling on a Play Station 2 or basketball on an XBox.

By Thursday I felt like I was making connections with the students. I helped a kid with his math and during Earned Activity Time I played pool with a student. A kid told me I looked like a detective, which I took as a compliment

I like having longer assignments. The first day I don't do very much. I only help if a kid asks for it, or I can see he/she is really struggling. Then I join them in a game during free time. By the middle of the second day they realize I'm not trying to pull some power trip with them and that I just want to help and they start to trust me, both with asking for help and with telling me about themselves. Then, when I ask them to stop talking or get to work they know I'm asking for a reason, not just because it's the rules.

By the end of the week I decided that I really liked this class, I was bonding with the kids and I thought I could do a lot of good here. Plus, I wanted to be there because the person I was subbing for is big in the hip-hop scene, and I thought it would be cool for the class to get a punk EA for a while. Unfortunately, I was sent elsewhere.

Kennedy High School
January 20

It was finals time. Since I couldn't help the kids with their tests, I ended up doing a lot of stupid busy work. For example, I had to take a multiple choice worksheet, cut out the answers, and paste them in a different order.

Kennedy High School
January 21

Today I worked in a class for kids who live in a group home. I didn't do much at first, looked up "cupola" for a kid. Two students couldn't get along. I took the more aggressive one to the school library, ostensibly to get newspapers for the class, but really to give him time to cool down away from the class. We walked slowly and talked a bit. He said he wasn't usually like that. I think he was trying to say something but didn't know how. I wished the walk back to the classroom was a couple blocks, but it was just a hall, and that's not enough time to let a kid know he can open up.

A kid had an X on his hands. Between classes I asked him if that meant he was straightedge. He seemed kind of impressed that I knew what straightedge was. When I told him I was straightedge, too, he flipped out. I told him at 29-years-old I've never had a beer or a cigarette. He was super excited. I told him I was vegan, too.

"I'm vegetarian! I want to go vegan! When I turn 16 and can get a job and can afford it I'm going to go vegan!" I asked him if he was into Minor Threat or Seven Seconds. He said no, he didn't really like punk; he was into hardcore. OK, I see I have my work cut out for me...

Most of the class went to the gym for the last period of the day. I stayed in the classroom with a kid who didn't want to go. I wrote in my journal and he made me an origami tiger. He was shy in handing it to me. And the student who I thought didn't like me asked if I was coming back tomorrow.

Kennedy High School
January 26-30

Though I was in the A-room primarily, the first period of everyday I went to help out in the Math Resource Room. I really enjoyed it and it strengthened my resolve to become a high school math teacher. And I think the kids appreciated having some guy who didn't tell them what to do but who was just genuinely excited to help them with math. On Wednesday I helped a girl with her assignment on place values. She asked if I was kind of a geek in school. "Not just kind of..." I said.

On Friday the teacher went around the room asking everyone what they were doing that weekend. I said my band was playing. The kids thought that was cool. "You should play here at school!"

"Naw, I think we're too loud."

"Then play outside."

Someone said as soon as my band recorded anything I had to bring it in for the class.

Mondale School
February 2 -March 5

The Mondale School is for high school kids who live in group homes. Students don't go there for four years, but rather one year, maybe just a few months, until they are placed in a foster home or released to their parents and transferred to another school. I had a good time in this room. The students seemed to be managing whatever setbacks they had been dealt really well. For the most part, they were kids I could get along with even if I wasn't getting paid to hang out with them. I really enjoyed working with the staff. There were two teachers and the principal. They had to be stricter with the students than other high schools as the students were a greater risk of running away or getting into trouble, but I feel they did an incredible job of balancing this out with giving the students a good amount of input on how the class was run and letting the students know their feelings and concerns were definitely taken into consideration.

When not giving general assitance in the classrooms, my main jobs were to make sure kids weren't talking about anything inappropriate (I was specifically looking out for drug and alcohol talk) and to keep tabs on everyone at lunch. Students could earn off campus priveleges, but they had to check out with me before they left and check back in when they returned. That meant I stood awkwardly in the cafeteria with a clipboard. After the first day I took a crossword puzzle with me so I had something to do while waiting for a student to check out. I think I weirded out the rest of the school. I was just some stranger looking around pensively and writing on this clipboard.

February 3

I think I won a kid's trust when I correctly identified Outkast coming from his headphones. Then one of the teachers and I took the kids to PE. As the Mondale School was a separate entity from the highschool it was housed in, we couldn't use their gym. We took the bus to the downtown YMCA every Tuesday and Thursday for PE. Today we played "Air Ball", which is kind of like volleyball but with a lighter ball and no net and almost no rules.

February 4

The straighedge kid from the class at Kennedy transferred here. During check-in, the principal had to talk to the kids about cracking down on people smoking during their off campus time. I flashed the kid the crossed arms straightedge sign.

During English, two girls talked about getting their tongues pierced, making not so subtle references to oral sex. I asked them to stop. "You know what we're talking about?" Kids always assume adults are totally ignorant of the things they've just found out about themselves, music, slang, nomenclature of deviant sexual acts. Sometimes I don't know if I should call them on it or not. Do I really want to let the kids know that I know what a bukkake video is? Probably not, but there's no way they can reasonably expect anybody not to know what they're talking about when they do the loose fist to mouth, tongue pushing the cheek gesture.

"Yes, I know what you're talking about."

"What?"

"...I can't say it." Then they teased me for blushing.

February 5

I played capture the flag during PE. One of the staff at the YMCA gave us a ride back in his van. The straightedge kid sat next to me. Two students in front of him asked what straightedge meant. "I don't drink, I don't do drugs, I don't smoke, I don't have premarital sex, I'm vegetarian... Dave's straightedge, too."

When I confirmed this, a girl asked, "You've never had sex?" I didn't know how to handle this. This was clearly none of their business and not an appropriate thing to ask, but if lead them to believe I've never had sex, all my cred is gone. I had to find a way to say I wasn't going to talk about it without coming across defensive. I'm not sure what I said, but the boy in front of me gave me a high five, so I'm pretty sure I know what they heard.

February 9

Before the students arrived, the two teachers, the principal, the administrator and I talked about whether students should be allowed to listen to music, specifically violent or sexist music. I got engrossed in the conversation and was ten minutes late in going out to pick up kids from the bus. As soon as I got out the classroom door I ran into the bus driver walking the students to the room. He looked so disappointed I felt horribly shamed.

At the end of the day I caught a girl changing her point sheet. That's a daily record of how they did academically and behaviorally throughout the day. I'm not sure what their homes do with them, but they take them. She changed it right in front of me and other students. Another student looked at her incredulously. She said, "Dave's not going to tell." At that point I had to tell the teacher. If I let a kid get away with that in front of another kid, I'm finished. Who's going to listen to anything I say after that?

The next morning the girl accused me of ratting her out. "Yeah, I had to." Somehow that answer satisfied her. She wasn't mad, which was a relief because she was a tough student who could definitely make me miserable if she wanted to.

February 17

A group of actors and writers called Playwrite came in and took five student from our class and five from the hearing impaired class. It was a two week program over the course of which the students would write a little one act play and the actors would perform it on the last day. I went with the kids for the first week and had to join in improv/get to know you games, which made me feel ridiculous. When the kids started writing, I wrote in my journal.

February 24

I ripped a little whole in my pants and got a scab on my knee hitting the floor while trying to get to the basketball before a 16-year-old kid. I'm pathetic.

March 1

There was a new girl. She had kind of a pre-genre punk style: a tie on her leg, a shirt with a fuzzy pink circle A on the sleeve and the word "PUNK" written in fuzzy letters and safety pinned on the back. I asked her what bands she likes, hoping I'd get a chance to talk about Bikini Kill. She said, "Pink Floyd... The Steve Miller Band..." The conversation ended there.

A teacher and I took the class to an African dance lesson at the ballet. I didn't want to dance but I had no choice. I felt pretty silly. I did a good job of avoiding myself in the mirror while dancing, but the few times I looked up, ugh.... A lot of kids came thinking they were just going to watch a dance and get credit for it. They were not into dancing at all and ended up sitting against the wall. The only thing that feels dumber than learning to dance with a group of 16-year-old boys is learning to dance with a group of 16-year-old boys watching you.

March 3

The whole class went on a field trip to watch a ballet. The students were more interested in it than I was. Then we went to a buffet, where I filled up on corn and french fries.

March 5

This was my last day here. The straightedge kid had a friend take a picture of both of us.

Kennedy High School
March 9

I was called to work one-on-one with a girl in a wheelchair. I showed up late and went to the math resource room to stow my coat and bike helmet. This was the class in which I subbed for a week in February. The kids seemed excited to see me. That doesn't happen often with high schoolers. They were disappointed I had to leave to meet my one-on-one in the art room. I sat next to her and wrote while she worked with clay. Her sister was interested by my writing. She showed me a bunch of poems she had written. They were of the "I was once in love" genre. I helped the whole class in her math classes. Last period I helped her write a story for English. It was fun.

Freeman Middle School
March 10

I had a rough day after work yesterday and I was considering not working today. But I need the money. When I picked the students up from the bus one girl asked who I was. "I'm Dave, I'm subbing for Ms. G." She burst into tears. Great, I've been here ten minutes and I've already ruined this kid's day.

The day got better. That girl burst into tears a couple times throughout the day. Not that that made the day better, it just meant it wasn't anything personal on me. Another kid kept acting up. In the middle of class he stood up and walked around, stopping in the doorway. I asked him to sit back down but he totally ignored me. I touched his shoulder. He got really upset and had to be taken to the detention room. When he came back half an hour later, I apologized for touching his shoulder but asked him to speak respectfully and tell me what's wrong and don't just flip out should something like that happen again. After that he was cool with me.

I took a student to his computers class where he practiced typing. I didn't realize I was supposed to bring a book with us for him to type from. We had to go back to class. He got upset because I wasn't going down the stairs the right way. I was supposed to be on the same step as him on the opposite foot.

Kennedy High School
March 12

I worked one-on-one with the same girl I worked with three days ago. Again, the students in the math resource room seemed glad to see me. As I walked down the hall to my student's art class I heard her sister tell her the sub was here. "Is it Dave? ...Yes!" She told me she was excited for me to help her finish the story we started a few days ago. I typed as she dictated.

Zulueta Middle School
March 31

I worked in the Behavior room today. Some of the kids recognized me from last year. That doesn't mean they liked me. Things went ok, I guess. I did a letter sound flash card game and read a book to the class. For my lunch break I went to the teachers' lounge, which was doubling as the ESL room. I sat tucked away in a corner where the students couldn't see me and read *Soldier's Pay*.

I was told my day ended at 3:30, even though the kids stayed until 3:45. As I was leaving a kid said he was going with me. I said I'd ride him doubles on the handle bars. "Oh, that's cold!" I didn't see how that was cold. A girl asked how could I ride a bike in slacks and cowboy boots. I lifted my pant leg to show her that I was wearing very classy vegan dress shoes, not cowboy boots. She instantly made fun of my purple socks, which were classy, too.

Hahn Middle School
April 1

Before class I found out the teacher grew up in a small town really close to the town where I grew up, and we were the same age. Luckily she had to meet the students at the buses before the "Did you know So-and-so?" game began. I was afraid I would have to admit I hadn't any friends in high school.

This was a class for middle school kids who live in group homes. It went really well. One of the kids transfered from another class in which I had subbed and was happy to see me. For most of the first half of the day I floated around the room helping kids with their math or reading and doing the New York Times crossword puzzle. One student told me his dad does crossword puzzles. Then he tried to do the puzzle. It doesn't sound like much, but he was definitely trying to bond with me.

I was left alone in the classroom to lead the Social Studies lesson. Things got a little unruly. A girl had the hiccups. When she wasn't paying attention I dropped a book on her table to try to scare them out of her. It didn't work, but the boy next to her let out a yelp so ridiculous it was worth it.

Arthur High School
April 6

One student was talking about when he hit puberty: "One day I woke up and looked down there... Oh my God!"

Freeman Middle School
April 16

At the end of the day the teacher in the special ed. room next door invited our class to join their party. Everyone got cookies and juice, then the teacher asked if anybody wanted to provide entertainment. A girl sang a quick song. Then someone put on a cd and four or five kids danced in front of the room. It was awesome. These kids had absolutely no self-consciousness at all, they were up there with huge smiles on their faces.

Keida Elementary School
April 19

I was sent to the kindergarten class. The day started out harmless enough. I helped kids make cards with glue and glitter and I played basketball at recess, which mostly involved me pretending to guard the kids then chasing down the airballs. Things took a turn for the worse when I had to change a kid's diaper. He was wriggly and restless so I had to change him standing up. He had already been changed once today, so I thought it wouldn't be so bad. I wasn't prepared for the sudden onslaught of stench and preponderance of shit. I almost puked. My eyes were watering and I was gagging as I pulled the diaper off and threw it in the garbage. As soon as he was free from his diaper, the kid ran to the toilet and flushed it. I took a second to compose myself, called him over and wiped. Judging from the constitency, this kid ate nothing but maple syrup and maybe flour. It was like he had sat in brown wheat paste. And now it was my job to clean him up. After every wipe the kid ran to the toilet and flushed it. It really stretched out a process I desperately wanted to speed up. After the fifth wipe I blocked him from getting to the toilet. He seemed to accept that his flushing time was over and backed into the wall, smearing shit on it. Within minutes there was an accompanying smear on the door. Soon he got restless and wanted this to be finished with, so he started moaning and flicking the lights on and off. I finally finished up and let the kid flush the toilet as a reward. A reward for what I'm not sure. I had him wash his hands while I cleaned the wall and door. When I washed my hands he ran over to the toilet and hugged it, resting his head on his arms on the rim. It grossed me out, but I was done. It wasn't going to kill him so we weren't going to spend time washing his arms. I had to get out of that bathroom. All in all, I guess it only took 15 minutes, but it felt much longer. In my mind I saw a clock with the hands spinning at an exaggerated speed; leaves of a page-a-day calendar were falling off and blowing away; babies were born, became adults, and grew grizzled and grey in the time it took me to change that diaper.

When I went back to class I wasn't the fun sub anymore. There was no more basketball, no playing with the kids during free time. Sorry, class, Teacher Dave is a broken man.

Freeman Middle School
April 21- 26

The first day was a little rough. There was a non-verbal autistic boy who was in the process of changing medication. He had been taken off his old meds and had to wait for them to pass out of his system before he could take the new. I felt really bad for the kid, he looked terrible. He had to realize something was going on with his body beyond his control and it had to freak him out. And to not have anyway to communicate what he needed or what he was feeling, I can't imagine how frustrating that would be. And to top it off he has to work with a stranger for a week. Not surprisingly, he had trouble with all this. He was really squirrelly and kept running around, darting out of the room and into other classes. The teacher took him and a few other kids on a field trip the first half of the day and I stayed behind and worked with two students on math.

After lunch I went with a couple students to their mainstream art class. The autistic kid ran into the room. I tried talking him into going back to his class to no avail. I know how to physically move kids in a way that's safe for both them and myself, but I didn't want to do that in front of the rest of the art class. Eventually I used a mix of safety holds and coaxing to get him to his class.

The next two days were easier, but only because the autistic kid was kept at home. The class went on a field trip to the mall on Friday. I know that doesn't sound very educational, but these were low functioning kids. Every Friday they take a field trip somewhere just to teach them how to behave and stay safe in public. I was in charge of two students. After lunch the teacher gave each student $1.50 to spend on a treat and we split up. One of my students bought a drink for $1, then asked if he could buy a cookie. I told him he didn't have enough money for a cookie. He spent 15 minutes asking the same question, not even bothering to change the wording.

I took my two students into a sporting goods store. They seemed content looking at the fishing gear and tents. They got more excited when they saw all the footballs and basketballs. Then they tried on shoes. I don't think the clerk was too thrilled with that, but I only let them try on floor models, I didn't make anybody get shoes from the back room. On the way out we passed a pogo stick. I didn't know they still made pogo sticks. For some reason I thought this would be the perfect time for me to try one for the first time. My first attempt didn't even last one jump. On my second attempt I fell flat on my back, all of my pocket change scattered on the floor around me. I twisted my ankle, too. I must have been in a good mood, because I remember thinking that must have looked funny. Luckily the kids' enjoyment of the situation was fleeting. They laughed a little, but by the time I stood up they were already asking if I would buy them a scooter or a skateboard.

shawn granton ★ 05/2004

The end

After spending the last few months putting this all together, culling four years worth of zines and journals, I feel like I have to ask myself why. What's the point of this? There's something fatalistic in reducing your life to a series of words. Like a photograph of a runner, all the motion and excitement is at best implied. Despite the visible signs of strain, the runner still lies idle, powerless on the page.

But still there's this pressing need to document, to leave tangible proof that, despite my dissatisfaction with the way things are going, I'm trying as hard as I can to lead a life I believe in. So here it is, a good chunk of the last four years of my life. You can judge for yourself how I managed with my sometimes embarrassingly earnest attempts at being at once ethical, optimistic and adult. Ideally I got better as I went along, but if not, as long as I err more on the side of doing what I think is right than doing what I think I'm supposed to, I can live with that.

And like I wrote in the introduction, I'm not trying to claim I'm great at what I do. The point of this is that I'm just a normal guy who was given this amazing job with no qualifications and no training and I'm trying to figure out how to do it as best I can. If anything in this book bothered you, please keep in mind I had no experience with any of this before I started. But if something bothered you please write to me. Especially any parents of children in special ed. or anybody who was or is in special ed. I could use all the help I can get in getting better at my job.

Conversely, if you liked anything in here, please write, too. I'd really like to hear from other alternative/anarchist teachers (especially math teachers) or from anybody who got anything out of this. Though I hope it was an enjoyable read, this isn't intended as just entertainment.

Dave
PO Box 12142
Portland OR 97212
poodrow@hotmail.com

Illustration credits

Aaron Renier did the illustration on page 61. Check out his beautiful comic, *Spiral Bound*, on Top Shelf.

Clutch did the illustrations on pages 20, 51, and 83. Write to him at PO Box 12409, Portland OR 97212 and ask about his comic *Clutch*. It's really, really good.

Nathan Beatty did the illustration on page 96. You should check out his comic *Brainfag* and his zine *Shrike*. www.brainfag.com

Keith Rosson did the illustration on page 39. You should order his book, *The Best of Intentions*, which compiles issues of his incredible zine *Avow*.

Nicole Georges isn't as mean as you might think, although she has been calling me Steve Urkel ever since I told her about the incident she illustrated on page 69 two years ago. You can get *Invincible Summer*, an anthology of her zines from Tugboat Press (PO Box 12409, Portland OR 97212) or from Microcosm.

Shawn Granton is a sophisticated man-about-town. When he's not helping other people out with their projects (like doing the illustration on page 120 for me) he works on his comic, Ten Foot Rule. Reach him at tfrindustries@scribble.com

All these comics and zines can be ordered through Microcosm. Also, nobody saw the students they drew, so any similarity to any real kid is coincidental.

Thanks

Joe Biel is an amazing person and an invaluable asset to the community. I feel lucky to count him among my friends and thank him deeply for his support and patience with me, without which this book would not exist. He and Alex Wrekk run Microcosm Publishing and Distribution, where you can also find their zines, The *Perfect Mix Tape Segue* and *Brainscan*, respectively.

Denise Ferguson not only gave birth to my friend Chad, but she so non-chalantly told me she wanted to read my book that I had no choice but to write one.

Thanks to Peter Shaver for the legal advice.

The following people deserve thanks for living what they believe and being constant sources of inspiration and friendship: Jonny, Jenna, Meghan, Candise, Moe, Erin Yanke, Erin Playman, Matt in Los Angeles, Bek, Lex, and all the Wollongong kids, Luke and the Melbourne kids, Kate and the Sheffield kids, Michelle and the Chicago kids, Travis and the Gainesvillians, everyone who put me up in the UK and Ireland (Willie, Natalia, and everyone at the warehouse in Dublin; Isy and Mike and the guy who recovered my stolen camera in Brighton; Dan and Matt in Manchester; Emma, Joe and Lachlan in Glasgow; Emma in Cardiff; Lisa and Ben in Bristol; Elvina in London; and Michelle and Sarah), and everyone who will put me up when I go to Canada and Alaska next year and Australia soon.

Special thanks to Mia for being an awesome niece.

And most importantly, thanks to my parents who have supported me in everything I've done. Mom and Dad, I love you

OK, here's a note about all the typos in the first printing. I'm sorry. You don't know how frustrated they made me. Things got rushed. Lawyers from the school district were threatening me and I decided I had to put it out right away or I'd chicken out. So I told Joe to print it and then I left town for two months. In the first printing I wrote:

Claire Barrera took on the unenviable task of proofreading this. Thanks are due to her for not only correcting my grammar and punctuation, but for giving criticism with coquettish honesty. And I still take the blame for any and all misplaced commas.

I feel I should repair any damage I've done to Claire's good name. I was doing rewrites while she was proofreading. I didn't have time to show her the new drafts. This time around more people have proofread, and I still take the blame for all misspellings, typos, misplaced commas, and other errata.

"Skipper"

Fig. 1 - My Bus Pass

Fig. 2: The photo ID I used to get a library card in Gainesville.